How a Rough-and-Tumble ~~~~~~ ~~~~~~
Dragged Me Back to Health ~~~~~

P9-DNU-742

Saved by Gracie

JAN DUNLAP

Authentic

Published by Authentic Publishers
188 Front Street, Suite 116-44
Franklin, TN 37064

Authentic Publishers is a division of
Authentic Media, Inc.

Library of Congress Cataloging-in-Publication Data
Dunlap, Jan
    Saved by Gracie : How a rough-and-tumble rescue dog dragged me back to health, happiness, and god / Jan Dunlap
    p. cm.
ISBN 978-1-78078-227-0
    978-1-78078-345-1 (eBook)

Printed in the United States of America
21 20 19 18 17 16 15 14   10 9 8 7 6 5 4 3 2

This book is for my husband, Tom,
and my daughter, Colleen,
who convinced me I could survive adopting a dog,
and for every person who has ever needed
a dog in their life, whether they knew it or not.

Contents

Acknowledgments

---

*F*irst and foremost, I want to acknowledge God's goodness in my life. I am awed and humbled by His unending generosity and love.

Much gratitude goes to my agent Greg Johnson who has opened new horizons for me as a writer. His faith that I will find the right publisher for my work sustains me and heartens me, and I am blessed by the companionship and tutelage of all the WordServe Literary authors and staff. Likewise, I feel that God has guided me to Kyle Duncan, my editor at Authentic, who has affirmed everything I hoped to achieve with telling this story.

I need to give a big round of applause to all my friends at Victoria's Three Rivers Parks dog park. Their encouragement, support, and friendship during my first year of living with Gracie helped me in countless ways as I learned to be a good dog owner. Cindy, Cori, Bridget, Rick, Eric, Jenni, Kristi, Leticia, Anne, Nancy, Kendra—I'll walk the big loop with you any day!

A special nod of thanks goes to all the animal rescue groups around the world who give so much of themselves to save animals. Your dedicated stewardship of God's creatures is a model and inspiration for us all.

As always, I owe a huge debt of gratitude to my husband and children, who always encourage and enable me to dream big dreams, and then help me to achieve them. Love you forever.

I'd been praying
pretty fervently to God
for the last year or so
to give me grace
to get my life back, but
I'd never imagined
His answer would
be so literal.
Not to mention a dog.

Introduction

Amazing Grace,
How sweet the sound
That saved a wretch like me.
I once was lost, but now am found,
Was blind, but now I see.

LYRIC FROM *AMAZING GRACE*
BY JOHN NEWTON (1725-1807)

It's early May, and I decide to buy a wading pool for our dog, Gracie. Since she's a black lab mix, she tends to get really hot when we walk her in the summer heat, and I think if she has a pool to lie in after our walks, she can cool down faster. Given that she also has nice big feet with claws, I figure that if a pool is going to survive more than one use, it can't be the inflatable kind. At seventy pounds, Gracie is a big girl, and "durable" is a requirement.

So I watch for the spring sale flyers that come in the newspapers, and as soon as I see a hard plastic wading pool advertised, I go to the store to get one.

"I need a pool for our dog," I explain to the saleswoman at the building supplies megastore as I study the four- and six-foot diameter pools on display in the garden center. If she thinks this is an unusual reason to purchase a child's wading pool, she doesn't show it.

I hold out my hands as a measure for Gracie's size and try to imagine our big black dog laying in a kiddie pool patterned with grinning red, yellow, and blue fish.

"She's too big to stretch out in the smaller one here," I announce to the saleswoman, "so I'll take the larger one."

I wrestle a pool off the top of the chest-high stack and awkwardly carry it to the cashier, trying not to knock over extensive floor displays of gas grills and weed-eaters along the way. As she rings it up, I realize that the hard-shell pool won't fit into the trunk of my Toyota Camry, so I ask her if someone could help me secure it to my car roof for the ride home. She assures me I can get help.

She's wrong.

Five minutes later, I'm still waiting for someone to help me with the pool. I find another cashier, who informs me that the store prohibits employees from helping customers strap items to their car roofs because of liability issues. She does offer me all the twine I want, however.

I look at the six-foot diameter pool laying on the parking lot asphalt next to my car. The circumference of the pool is bigger than the car's roof.

"I can do this," I tell myself, heaving the pool on top of my car and beginning to thread the twine over the pool and through my car windows. By the time I'm done, it looks like a monster spider has spun a web over my car.

No problem. The pool is secure.

Until my car speed reaches 15 mph.

Then the pool bucks and shudders on my roof and begins to slide sideways. I quickly roll down my window and stick my arm up and over the edge of the roof to grab the edge of the pool. Every time the wind catches it, I feel like I'm holding onto a tie-down attached to a hot air balloon that wants to take off my arm. I wonder how much torque it would take to pull my arm from my shoulder socket. I hit my emergency flashers, pull off the road and tighten the twine. I take back roads home, drive under ten miles per hour, and keep my flashers on.

"Gracie better appreciate this," I mutter as I inch home. And then the twine breaks with a loud snap, and in the rear-view mirror, I watch the pool gracefully fly off the car and land in the middle of the road behind me.

Thankfully, the road is empty and no oncoming car has been attacked by my dog's smiley fish motif wading pool. I pull over again, turn off the car and walk back to retrieve the pool.

"I cannot believe I am doing this," I say out loud as I lift the six-foot diameter pool off the road and return to the car. I examine my twine, which is now shredded into several pieces, and debate what to do.

Option #1: I can abandon the pool on the side of the road in hopes some mom with a carload of hot and crabby little kids will find it, at which point the ecstatic mom will praise God for miraculously answering her prayers, and take it home.

Option #2: I can leave it and come back with heavy rope to secure it to the roof. Maybe then I'd be able to maintain a car speed of ten miles an hour and make it home before nightfall.

Option #3: I can just forget the whole thing and abandon the pool. But then I would be throwing away the money—all of ten dollars—I'd spent on it. Not to mention littering. How much of a fine do you get for discarding a pool on the side of the road?

I don't know and don't want to find out. I grab the pool and stuff it into my trunk as far as it will go. The hard plastic gives just enough—probably a result of bucking the headwinds on the roof of the car—so I can finally fold it over. A third of it still hangs outside my trunk, so I take the longest twine piece I can find and tie the trunk shut over the pool. I drive home slowly, all the while thinking that Gracie better LOVE this pool.

Guess what?

She doesn't. She refuses to get into it. She drinks water out of it, but she won't set foot in it. If I'd wanted to get her a water dish for outside, I'm sure I could have found something a lot smaller that I wouldn't have had to tie to the top of my car. What am I going to do with a six-foot diameter wading pool?

I take off my sandals and step into the pool. I have to admit it feels pretty darn good on a hot spring day. I walk around in a little circle, enjoying the swish of the cold water against my ankles. A glass of iced tea would be a nice touch, I decide. I grab a book and a lawn chair and leave my feet cooling in the pool while Gracie lies in the shade beside it.

A pool. A cold drink. A dog.

Life is good.

"Hey, Gracie," I tell her, "I could get used to this. The pool's a great idea. Thanks for sharing."

And thanks be to God . . . for answered prayer.

Because the fact is, I'd been praying pretty fervently to God for the last year or so to give me grace to get my life back, but I'd never imagined His answer would be so literal.

Not to mention a dog.

One morning,
I woke up and my
chest hurt.
I couldn't seem to draw
a deep breath, and
I wondered why someone
had left an elephant
on top of me.

I never wanted a dog

I never wanted a dog.

But there I was, staring at a two-year-old black lab mix at an adoption event at our local pet store. My husband and sixteen-year-old daughter had just taken the dog for a quick walk around the adjacent strip mall, and I could tell the decision had already been made.

This dog was coming home with us.

It was going to shed on my sofa, scratch my wood floors, stink up my house and never allow me to eat in peace again. Despite my daughter's promises to take the dog for all the walks, give it all the grooming, and prepare all its meals, I knew, without a doubt, the dog would end up as my responsibility. With less than two years to go before I finally became an empty-nester after thirty years of raising children, the last thing I wanted was to take on a rescued dog with unknown needs and issues.

And did I mention that I'd been afraid of dogs my whole life?

Especially big black ones?

"I've always kind of wanted a dog," my husband quietly commented to me.

I gave up the stare-down with the dog and handed my husband our checkbook to pay the adoption fee.

"Does she have a name?" I asked the woman from the animal shelter who was filling out the paperwork as fast as she could. I wondered if she was afraid we'd change our minds before she got it done.

"Gracie," she told us. "She can shake hands, she's good on the leash, and she loves people. She'll jump a fence to get to you."

Okay, I thought, so the dog is loyal. I'd always heard that about dogs. It was supposed to be one of their best qualities.

"But she doesn't like cats," the woman added. "She barks at cats."

That wouldn't be a problem for us. Our cat had died of kidney failure the previous Christmas. I'd actually promised myself that it would be my last pet, since I'd taken it so hard when she died. I had five fabulous children, a wonderful husband, a college teaching job, a budding writing career, speaking engagements, and with any luck, grandkids in the years to come. I wasn't looking for a furred companion.

But my third daughter, my last child at home, had worn me down with her pleas for a dog.

"As soon as I have my own place, I'll take her with me," Colleen vowed. "If you can just take care of her while I'm at college, that's all you'll have to do, Mom. I promise. Just a few years. She'll make me feel safe."

Ah, yes. The feeling of being safe. The assurance that life is good, and everything will turn out well. The belief that life is fair, and that if you do all the right things, God will keep you safe.

I used to believe that, until a medical diagnosis turned my life upside-down.

To be completely accurate, it was a medical *mis*diagnosis, but it still threw me for the biggest loop of my life.

One morning, I woke up and my chest hurt. I couldn't seem to draw a deep breath, and I wondered why someone had left an elephant on top of me.

I opened my eyes and looked

No elephant.

I poked my husband Tom in his side.

"What is it?" he asked, still half asleep.

"My chest hurts and I can't catch my breath," I told him.

We went to the local emergency room, where the nurses hooked me up for heart monitoring. When I explained that my mother had had a history of heart disease and stroke, they handed me a nitroglycerin tablet to dissolve under my tongue, which ER protocol prescribes for someone having a heart attack.

A heart attack.

WHAT?

I was fifty-one years old, I didn't smoke, rarely drank, and exercised regularly. I got my colonoscopy, my full-body skin cancer check, and my mammograms on a regular basis, and I always read the monthly bulletin from our clinic. I thought I was in great health, but at that moment, I experienced a shattering revelation: I was going to die.

Of course, I'd always known it intellectually, but I'd always thought of it as an event so far in the future, that it was really pretty irrelevant to my daily routine. Lying in an emergency room cubicle with a nitroglycerin tablet under my tongue, though, went a long way toward making the idea of death a lot more immediate.

And scary.

Very scary.

It was even scarier than reading the expiration date on the bottle of salad dressing I'd used at dinner, only to find out it expired a year ago.

I was going to die.

My heart, however, checked out fine, as far as the emergency room doctors could determine. They kept me in the hospital overnight for observation, and I went home the next day, promising to schedule a stress test with my clinic as soon as possible. Relieved beyond words, I concluded that nothing was amiss since the doctors released me to go home. My fears were clearly unfounded and my chest pains, a physical fluke.

The Grim Reaper wasn't coming for me yet, after all.

Three weeks later, though, I experienced a thudding in my chest. Remembering my promise to take a stress test, I called the clinic and made an appointment. I ran on the treadmill while a cardiologist and two interns watched. Two days later, my doctor called with the news that the stress test result came back positive.

"You need to see a cardiologist," he told me while I tried to make sense of what he was saying. "You need to do it right away."

Confused and frightened by the sudden urgency and concern in his voice, I saw a cardiologist the next day.

"We need to find out what's going on with your heart," the doctor explained. "When we have a positive stress test result, we anticipate there is a blockage, and if there is a blockage in your artery, you'll need a stent. And the only way we can know that for sure is to do an angiogram. With your family history, we don't want to take any chances."

I took the soonest available slot for an angiogram.

Three days passed before my procedure. My anxiety levels soared. I was afraid I was going to drop dead any moment. I measured my pulse constantly while I waited for my angiogram and the possible insertion of a stent. I couldn't sleep . . . mostly because I kept taking my pulse. I tried to imagine what kind of recovery a stent would require.

But it never happened.

The angiogram was clean. There was a little calcification along one artery, but nothing that required intervention. My stress test had produced a false positive, which, the heart surgeon explained to me, happens 15% of the time. I was in the lucky 15%. I could resume all my good habits and enjoy great health well into my twilight years. No problem.

Except that something tagged along home with me from the hospital.

Uncertainty.

If trained doctors could make a mistake in thinking I had a heart problem, couldn't they also err in the other direction? Hadn't I, along with most other Americans, seen enough television programs about missed diagnoses to know that the expertise of medical professionals wasn't infallible? As an educated woman who'd been brought up to respect the knowledge and authority of doctors when it came to my physical being, I suddenly felt adrift.

If my body could malfunction and doctors couldn't say what was wrong, where did that leave me?

Watching Dr. Oz?

Except that I don't have a television.

Or any medical training.

Which meant I only had one option: I had to rely on God, and trust that I really was okay.

Which should have worked, but didn't. Every time I committed myself to giving up all my fears to God, I sabotaged myself by continually taking it back—piece by piece—a little while later. Even the four years I'd spent studying the Word of God in my theology master's degree program wasn't enough to break through my stubborn conviction that I was in charge of my mortal life.

"I am the master of my fate: I am the captain of my soul." If William Ernest Henley hadn't penned those words in his poem "Invictus," I would have. In modern America, those words are practically the national mantra.

Yet they are directly opposed to what Jesus Christ teaches us. We are in God's hands, thanks to His saving sacrifice.

The problem was, I kept jumping out of those loving hands.

I worried about my health. I didn't want to do anything that might risk my physical safety. I didn't want to be out of the house for any length of time, exposed to crowds and strangers and unpredictability. In my obsession to preserve my life, I was afraid of trying anything new and unexpected.

Until I saw a mental health counselor. That was certainly something new for me. My doctor thought it might help me with my growing anxiety, so I read the books she recommended. I repeated affirmations and positive self-talk. I continued to pray, out of habit, out of desperation, for healing, for help, for grace.

I wanted my old life back.

But in some ways, part of me had already died. I was developing a full-fledged anxiety disorder, and it was shaping me into a different person.

A person who was afraid to live.

So when my daughter said she wanted to feel safe, I understood. What was worse, I was afraid her fear was born of my own.

In that moment, I decided if a dog could save Colleen from living with the fear that was eating away at me, then I would learn to live with a dog for her sake. Or I would, at least, make an effort.

"If she already responds to the name Gracie," I said, "let's keep it. The less confusion, the better."

But if I had been honest, I would have admitted that not giving the dog a new name was just another safety-net strategy on my part: by not naming her, I could maintain a safe emotional distance from the animal. I was, after all, afraid of dogs—always had been. If, as I fully expected, the newest member of our family didn't work out, if I couldn't tolerate a dog in my house, it would be easier for me to return her to the shelter if I hadn't named her myself. Naming was too personal; it implied a commitment I didn't feel.

"Gracie it is," my husband agreed.

And that was how Gracie, the rescued dog, came to live with us.

What I never expected, though, were all the ways she would come to rescue me.

And who, except for God, who knows our hearts better than we do ourselves, would have come up with a plan like that?

Chapter 2

A mistake of epic proportions

"Stop licking the couch!" Colleen and I shout in unison from our seats at the kitchen counter, our eyes on our laptop screens.

Behind us, in the living room, Gracie is sprawled in her usual spot on the loveseat, giving herself a noisy bath. After sixteen months with Gracie, my daughter and I can distinguish the difference by the sound alone when she is licking the furniture cushions instead of her fur. My guess is that our shared familiarity with the dog's bathing sounds constitutes some kind of bonding experience for us, because we immediately catch each other's eye and laugh.

My daughter and me, not me and the dog.

As for the furniture-watering behavior, I don't know why Gracie licks the cushions. At first I thought it was that her tongue was just so big, it couldn't help but drag across the furniture as she bathed her limbs and belly. Now I think it's some kind of habit she's developed. Maybe there's some kind of chemical in the fabric that tastes good to her, or is addictive. Or maybe the rhythmic stroking of her tongue against the texture of the cushions is as soothing to her as it appears to be for a man who continually smooths his fingers over a long mustache.

Given the choice, I think I'd tolerate the licking behavior better. At least I could tell myself, "She's a dog. She doesn't know any better." I think that sounds more compassionate than "He's a man. He doesn't realize how stupid he looks playing with his facial hair. You don't see me playing with my facial hair, do you?"

Well, actually, you probably could if you caught me between chin-waxings. Sometimes I can feel a tiny stub of whisker, and it about drives me crazy, so I keep rubbing my knuckles against it.

Is that too much information?

At least I don't lick the couch.

When you don't have pets in the house, furniture stays clean for a fairly long time. When you do have furred pets, they leave hair all over the place. And if you have pets that go outside, you can add grass and mud to the layers of dirt and dust that quietly accumulate on every floor and surface in your home. I'd never been obsessive about germs or cleanliness—I did raise five children, remember—but I couldn't stand seeing animal hair left on furniture I was expected to use whenever I visited friends with dogs. It just confirmed my observation that dogs are filthy animals and that I never wanted one in my home.

That being said, I'd at least had the foresight to bring a towel with us in the car when we drove to the pet store on adoption day.

Just in case.

"We'll spread it over the backseat if we end up bringing home a dog today," I explained to Tom while we waited for Colleen to join us in the car. "Now, I'm not expecting we'll be doing that," I quickly added. "There are a lot of dogs available for adoption, and this is only our first look. I don't want us to feel like we have to choose a dog today from among the ones we see here. We have lots of time to make this decision."

All the while, I was praying. "Oh, Lord, please don't let us find a dog today. I really don't want a dog. I'm afraid of dogs. I don't need a dog in my life. I'm just going along with this to make Colleen happy. That will be enough, won't it?"

And yet, I knew how my husband operated. Once Tom began to consider something, it might as well have been a done deal. For the thirty-plus years of our marriage, that knowledge of his behavior had served me well.

"Where would your dream vacation spot be?" I'd asked him two years earlier, completely sure that wherever it was, we'd be there within months.

"Costa Rica," he'd replied without a moment of hesitation.

"I wonder what it would cost?" I'd mused.

"I don't know," he'd said. "It would be interesting to find out."

Nine months later, we were in Costa Rica, enjoying the trip of a lifetime.

So I knew exactly how perilous it was, driving to an adoption day at the local pet store.

Especially given his comments a few days earlier. Colleen and I had been browsing online canine adoption sites in my misguided—make that *inane*—hope that looking at dog photos would be sufficiently gratifying for her. Hearing us comparing dogs, Tom peered over our shoulders and wistfully remembered the series of dogs his family had owned when he'd been a young boy.

I say "series" of dogs because none of them lasted very long; runaways and run-overs seemed to be the fate of all dogs in his childhood experience. Perusing the online photos of dogs, though (unmistakably happy faces, every one), Tom mused: "Gee, I wonder what it would be like to have a dog that didn't run away or get hit by a car?"

"Oh, Dad," my daughter said, her eyes beginning to tear up in sympathy. "That is so sad."

I gave Tom the evil eye.

He slid me a smile and shrugged his shoulders. "It's the truth. I'd consider thinking about getting a dog now."

As you might imagine, after that little exchange, there was no way I was letting Tom and Colleen go to the pet store without me. Though I plainly saw the odds stacking up against me and my wishes, I honestly believed that as long as I could put in my two cents' worth of objection, and find fault with as many dogs as were there, I still had a chance at averting dog ownership.

The reality, however, is that while I may have had anxiety issues, I was no slacker in the denial department, either. Despite my daughter's fervent desire, my husband's agreement to "think" about getting a dog, and my own protective instincts to do what was right for my child, I still didn't imagine I would actually have a dog for a pet. From everything I'd ever read or heard from friends, dogs took time, work, and attention that I didn't have—or want—to give. Dogs were messy. Dogs liked to roll in dead things. Dogs were obnoxious when you had company.

What I hadn't accounted for, however, was how heart-pulling a pair of big brown eyes could be—especially when those eyes were at one end, and on the other end was an ecstatically wagging tail, as said dog looks out at you from the inside of a big wire crate. And when you realize this animal is all alone in the world, abandoned, unwanted and unloved, how can you not see hope itself burning in those eyes—hope that, finally, HERE is the person who will take you home forever?

"You can take her for a walk outside the store," the adoption volunteer enthusiastically said as she drew the dog out of its cage and thrust its leash into my daughter's hands. "You can get to know her that way, and see what you think."

By the time I opened my mouth to say that wouldn't be necessary, that we were just looking today and not adopting, Tom, Colleen, and the dog were already outside the store, walking away from me on the sidewalk. I trotted to catch up with them.

"How do you know what to do?" I asked my daughter.

"You just hold on to the leash," my husband answered for her. "It's not rocket science."

"But this dog is big," I countered. "What if she decides to start running? She could drag Colleen into the street. She could get hit by a car."

I remembered Tom's dog history from a few nights back. "Tom, you of all people know that dogs get hit by cars. And if she's dragging Colleen, then Colleen could get hit by a car. *You* could get hit by a car."

"I'm not going to get hit by a car, Mom," my daughter assured me.

"You don't know that," I insisted.

"No one's going to get hit by a car," Tom patiently pointed out. He took my arm and let Colleen and Gracie get a little ahead of us. "You're overreacting, Jan," he said quietly. "We're just taking her for a walk. The dog isn't planning on making an escape, nor does it have a death wish."

"You don't know that," I repeated sullenly.

"Look at Colleen," he said.

I watched my daughter stop at the corner of a sidewalk. The dog stopped beside her. Together, they crossed the street to a grassy area. My daughter's eyes were glued on the dog, happiness beaming from her face. I could have sworn she stood up straighter.

"She likes walking her," my husband continued. "I don't think it would be a bad thing for her to take on the responsibility of a dog. It would build confidence."

It would make her feel safe.

The magic words rose unbidden in my mind, reminding me of how we'd gotten to this point of looking at dogs for adoption. I wanted Colleen to be free of the fear that, well, dogged me. I looked again at my daughter and the black lab mix.

Gracie walked obediently at Colleen's side. When Colleen stopped, Gracie sat on her haunches and gazed adoringly at my daughter. When Colleen resumed moving, Gracie matched her pace, a bright bounce in her walk, her ears perked, her head up, her black tail curled in a perfect circle that left the tip resting lightly on her back. If Gracie had been a little larger, she could pass for a show pony, I thought.

A show pony that was going to live in my house.

I gave myself a mental head slap.

What was I thinking when I agreed to come here? Of course, we were going to bring a dog home today. I even brought the stupid towel for the back seat!

We signed the papers and Colleen led Gracie to the car in the parking lot.

"We don't have a kennel for her to ride in," I observed. "Doesn't she need to be restrained, or something? You know, like a child? Oh my gosh—I hope she's not afraid of riding in a car."

Colleen opened the door to the back seat, and Gracie hopped in, walked to the far side of the bench seat and promptly planted her backside. She solemnly looked at the three of us outside the car.

"I guess she's ready to roll," my husband said.

We climbed in and pulled out of the lot. Gracie looked out the window, then turned toward Colleen, her long muzzle sniffing delicately at my daughter's face. A few minutes later, Colleen let out a quiet "Oh!" from the back seat. I turned to look.

Gracie had scooted closer to Colleen and laid her head in my daughter's lap.

"We're taking you home, Gracie," Colleen whispered.

My husband took a look at the two of them in the rear view mirror. "She's going to be a good dog," he assured me.

"We'll see," I said, grappling with the reality that we had bought a dog and were, indeed, at that very moment, in the process of bringing it into our home and into our lives. I envisioned dirty furniture, random barking, gnawed woodwork, and terrified UPS men who would never again leave an item on our front step.

I can't do this, I told myself. *This is a mistake of epic proportions.*

And then a piece of scripture popped into my head. For years, it had hung on my children's bedroom wall, illustrated by a wide-eyed child watching a butterfly emerge from a cocoon.

With God, nothing is impossible.

Out of desperation, I grabbed onto it and prayed all the way home in the car. *I can't do this, God, but I know that with You, nothing is impossible, right? I mean, I thought I was going to die because of my stress test, but I didn't. I thought it was impossible for the doctors to be wrong about that, but you showed me that wasn't true. So, now, I'm asking for this—please help me live with this dog.*

Of course, being obsessed with control and still questioning my relationship with God in the midst of my ongoing anxiety, I couldn't help adding (as if God needed instruction from me!), *In fact, if You can just keep the dog away from me, I think I'll be able to deal with it.*

I didn't know then that dogs are called "companion" animals for a very good reason.

Unfortunately, not everyone who thinks they want a companion animal can actually keep one.

(Note that I could mention again here a certain person's family track record. But I won't.)

According to Sharon Annette McCuddy, life-long dog owner and author of the online "Lucky Dog" series, there are four primary sets of reasons that dogs end up in shelters: unrealistic expectations of owners, changed lifestyle, legal issues, and stray/rescue/cruelty situations. According to the Humane Society of the United States, approximately 5 million cats and dogs were taken into animal shelters in 2012; of those animals, half were given up by owners and half brought in by animal control. The statistics also show that, every year, roughly one-third of the animals in shelters will be adopted, while the rest are euthanized, and a full 20 percent of the adopted dogs will wind up back in the shelters.

That's a whole lot of unwanted companions sitting in American animal shelters.

Our Gracie was no exception. Based on the paperwork the rescue organization provided, originally Gracie had been picked up as a stray puppy in Missouri, then adopted by a woman who was later reported to animal control authorities for animal cruelty. When the authorities came to check on Gracie, she was locked in a basement, emaciated, and covered in her own feces. She was taken out of the home and returned to a rescue group who nursed her back to health. That group folded, but was able to place Gracie with another shelter organization in Minnesota. By the time we met her, Gracie was two years old and had been in and out of several shelters and foster homes on her way to Last Chance (I kid you not—the name of the shelter was Last Chance), the group that brought her to the adoption event.

The adoption volunteer who had been fostering Gracie since her arrival in Minnesota only gave us one caution: the dog would do anything for food and could be aggressive if other dogs were around while she ate. Given her history, I wasn't surprised. If I'd been starved in a basement, I'd be pretty darn possessive of my food, too.

I made a mental note to be sure not to eat in front of the dog.

Exactly how we were going to manage that, I had no idea, because there was no way I was going to lock up this dog anywhere after what she had already endured. Having successfully raised five children to eat fairly regularly and politely, I was pretty sure we could also teach a dog a feeding routine that we could all live with. Besides, if the volunteer was correct, Gracie would do anything for food, which meant we had an easy way to reward good behavior. How hard could it be to train a dog that was hungry for both food and love?

A piece of cake, I told myself.

Ignorance is a wonderful thing, isn't it?

There weren't
a hundred accidents
or vicious animals
waiting for me in
the woods.
Instead, there was
the spring smell
of the earth,
the trickling sound
of the stream, birds
calling, buds opening.
It was beautiful.

Chapter 3

An unexpected adventure

A few months after Gracie came home to live with us, I was looking online for obedience classes, and stumbled onto a wealth of advice tips to make a dog's entrance into its new home less stressful.

I read through the list with growing dismay.

We hadn't done a single one.

1. *When you bring your new dog home, immediately take it for a leash walk around the neighborhood. This will help the dog acclimate itself to new surroundings, and perhaps burn off some of the stress it is probably feeling in a new and strange environment.*

As soon as we got home, my daughter walked Gracie into the house. None of us even considered taking her outside for a walk since she'd conveniently relieved her bladder during the short walk outside the pet store. Gracie looked around the room, looked at us, and made a beeline for the couch.

"No," my daughter, my husband, and I firmly said in unison. At least we'd done that much right—decided on house rules for the dog—on our way home. According to the list of advice, though, we should have had that discussion long before we went to get a dog, not on the ride home with the dog already in the car.

Whatever. Gracie heeded our command and didn't jump on the couch.

"She listens to us," I said in surprise. "That's a good thing."

"Come on, Gracie," my daughter said to the dog. "I'll show you our room."

The two of them walked away to Colleen's bedroom. I noted that the dog didn't eat the walls, tear up the furniture, lose control of her bladder or bowels, or attack my child.

"It's going to be fine," my husband assured me again.

If the dog was overstressed by unfamiliar surroundings and needed to burn off energy, she sure didn't show it. So much for the first piece of advice I hadn't known to take.

2. *Prepare ahead of time to welcome a new member into your family. Have dog food and a water dish ready, along with a few toys to entertain your new dog.*

My husband brought in the extra-large bag of dog kibble that we had purchased at the store. I searched through the cupboards and found an empty ice-cream bucket to use for water, filled it half-way, and set it on the floor in a corner of the kitchen. Another search yielded an unused pie plate which I figured would work as a food dish until I could buy one more suitable. That is to say, one with tall sides to keep the food from spilling all over the floor. The last thing I wanted was to be crunching dry dog food under my feet every time I walked into the kitchen. It was bad enough I'd let a dog into our house, but I didn't want to be reminded of it with each step I took.

Dog toys? We didn't have any. I added it to my shopping list, hoping that the dog would restrain herself from appropriating all the shoes and pillows in the house until I could get her a designated dog toy.

> 3. *Take the dog to her crate and let her sniff around it. Encourage her to enter and stay in the crate and provide her with a treat to reward her when she does so. Stay with her constantly, and gradually allow her into additional rooms.*

Crate? What crate? Not only did we not have dog dishes, we didn't have a crate for her to sleep in at home. Colleen wanted Gracie to sleep in her room, and I sure wasn't putting a dog kennel in a bedroom.

Dog bed—and treats—were added to my shopping list.

As for gradually allowing the dog into additional rooms, that was unknown advice to me, too. Within the first ten minutes of

Gracie's arrival, Colleen gave the dog the complete home tour. Apparently Gracie approved, because I didn't hear any snarls of disgust or dog laughter at my limited skill in interior design. Afterward, when Colleen sat down at the computer to tell her friends about her new dog, Gracie must have figured she was on her own, because the next thing I knew, there was a big black dog panting at me while I folded laundry in my bedroom.

"You can't come in here," I told the dog in my sternest voice. She was blocking the door out of my room, and I felt panic rising, realizing that I was alone facing this dog named Grace. Did she smell my fear? Was she baring her teeth at me?

"Out," I said, a slight tremor in my voice. I waved my hands at her, praying she wouldn't interpret my gesture as threatening and decide to lunge at me with her big muzzle. I was folding laundry; I didn't want blood on the clean clothes.

Lunging, however, was not her style.

Instead, she threw herself on the floor at my feet and rolled onto her back, her long skinny legs sticking up in the air as she writhed on the floor and exposed her teeth.

"Someone come get this dog!" I yelled, totally terrified by the size of her teeth and her manic movements. If I'd had any doubt before about having a dog in the house, I was absolutely convinced now that I couldn't live with it. "She's being aggressive with me!"

My husband appeared in the doorway. Gracie immediately stood up and assumed a submissive stance, head and tail down.

I told Tom what had happened. He looked from me to the dog and then back at me again.

"I think she wants to play with you," he said.

"I thought she was going to bite me," I countered. "I'm not going to be afraid in my own home," I insisted. "We're going to have to take her back."

Colleen appeared beside my husband.

"Please, Mom, can't we just give it a little time? This is all new to Gracie, too." She stroked the dog's ears and Gracie lifted her head, her tail curving up again.

I swear the dog smiled.

I let out a big sigh.

"All right. I'll try. But you keep an eye on her, Colleen. She's your dog, not mine," I reminded her. "And I don't want her in my room. I want at least one room in this house where she can't go."

A room where I can feel completely safe, I added silently.

"Okay, we won't allow her in our room," Tom agreed. He moved aside and Gracie followed Colleen out. "She's not going to hurt you, Jan," he insisted. "You just have to get used to each other."

Not going to happen, I silently added again. *She's a dog, and I'm not.*

So much for tip #3 about bringing the dog home.

4. *Keep your dog on a leash in the house for the initial transition into her new home.*

Nope. Never even occurred to us. As soon as Gracie crossed the threshold into our home, she was off leash. I'll never forget the expression on our vet's face when I took Gracie in for her first checkup five days after we adopted her.

"How's she doing when you're out of the house?" he asked.

"Pretty good so far," I told him. "She chewed up Colleen's sunglasses the first time we left her alone in the house, and I think she gnawed a little on the corner of our coffee table in the living room, but other than that, she hasn't hurt anything."

He looked at me blankly.

"And I was gone for three hours this morning, and when I got home, she was just lying on the couch, although I noticed that my slipper was sitting on the floor where I hadn't left it."

His mouth fell open and he stared at me. "You don't put her in a kennel when you leave her alone?"

His incredulous tone stopped me cold.

"Am I supposed to?"

Talk about clueless.

Come Monday morning, Gracie had been in our home for less than 42 hours when I found myself alone with her.

Really alone.

Colleen caught the bus to school, and Tom went to work at the office. Since Colleen had walked Gracie before leaving for the day, I figured I had until noon before I had to take her out again. In the meantime, I could do my regular Monday morning routine of lifting my hand weights and teaching my online classes. The dog hadn't attacked me yet, so I decided if I just acted like I wasn't afraid of her, she wouldn't smell my fear and tear me limb from limb.

What I didn't account for was that she didn't want to let me out of her sight. (Remember that "companion animal" comment I made earlier?)

I walked into the kitchen to clean up the breakfast dishes.

She followed me in and watched.

I went downstairs to lift weights.

She sat behind me on the floor.

I went to use the bathroom.

She waited outside the door.

I'd been handed a new job, I realized: I was now a dog's security blanket.

I recalled the background information the adoption volunteer had shared, and reminded myself that this dog loved people so much, she'd jump a fence to be with a human. Compared to that, following me around the house must have been a walk in the park for her.

Well, not exactly a walk in the park, I hoped, since the park, and not the house, was where I expected her to toilet. The last thing I wanted was to send the dog mixed signals.

I had to admit that Gracie's apparent need to be around me all the time did make sense in light of the volunteer's assessment of the dog's desire to attach to a person. At the moment, however, I preferred she not have to do any jumping at all to prove her loyalty—or anything else, for that matter. If she got up on her hind legs, she'd be as tall as I was, but her teeth were much bigger than mine.

So, despite my conviction that I would never welcome a dog in my life, I became determined to give this one what she'd never had: a person she could trust. As those first (nerve-wracking) hours passed with Gracie accompanying me soundlessly everywhere I went in our home, I began to believe that I could at least do this much for her: be a kind presence. I summoned my courage and stuck my hand out to her slowly and let her sniff my knuckles.

"Good girl," I told her. I turned my hand over and she sniffed my palm, her big nose snuffling loudly.

She didn't bite me.

"Okay," I said, letting out the air I didn't know I was holding.

Her ears pricked up and her tail wagged.

Now what? I wondered. I remembered my husband's words.

"Here's the deal, Gracie," I told the dog. "We just have to get used to each other. We don't have to be crazy about each other, we just have to get along. I think I can manage that. Maybe," I added, considering again her size and dogness.

Her brown eyes swung to the front door, then back to me. I looked at the clock in the living room and saw that it was noon.

Was she expecting someone?

Since no one had mentioned that she was able to use the phone or send an email, I had to assume that a visitor was not imminent.

Again, she looked at the door, and then at me.

She panted, her big brown eyes locked on mine.

She needed to go out.

And I'd have to take her.

I had to walk the dog.

A moment of near-panic set in.

I had to walk a dog!

All weekend, my daughter had performed the dog-walking function. Since we lived in a townhome, we didn't have a private yard, let alone an enclosed one, which meant that whenever Gracie needed to go outside, she had to be accompanied. I'd even used that argument repeatedly with my daughter when we'd discussed adopting, but she was adamant that she wanted to walk—had, in fact, been *wanting* to walk—in our neighborhood, but hadn't felt comfortable doing it alone. A dog, Colleen insisted, would give her a sense of protection and enable her to get the exercise we both agreed would be good for her.

In theory, it made a lot of sense.

In reality, my brain conveniently overlooked the fact that the dog might not be willing to always wait to walk until Colleen was available.

As a result, I had yet to put a leash on Gracie and walk out the door with her. Now, however, in the face of the inevitable first walk, possible scenarios of disaster sprang to life in my head.

Disaster #1. She would attack the first person we saw on the sidewalk, and I wouldn't be able to pull her off. We'd need to call an ambulance, and I'd end up in court being sued by the victim.

Disaster #2. She would strain so hard at her end of the leash that I would lose my footing and she would drag me around the block on my face.

Disaster #3. She'd see a squirrel and bolt after it, the leash torn from my fingers.

Disaster #4. She'd run into the street and almost cause a car accident, and it would be my fault for being an inept dog owner.

Disaster #5. She'd slip out of her leash and run away, and even though I had no control over it, my daughter would blame me for losing her dog on purpose. She would hate me forever.

Disaster #6. The dog would get killed, either because it ran away from me directly into the path of a car, or because another dog attacked it and I was unable to pry them apart.

Pry them apart? I'd be so paralyzed with terror, I'd run screaming back to the house. No way would I ever approach two snarling dogs, let alone try to separate them.

Gracie looked at the front door again, then back at me. She barked once.

It didn't matter if disaster was waiting on the other side of the door; Gracie had to go outside, and I was the only person available to take her there.

"I can do this," I muttered to myself in order to pluck up my courage. "If dogs ran to their death or killed someone every time they went outside, no one would have dogs, right?"

Or they wouldn't have them very long.

A certain family came into mind . . .

I immediately stopped thinking about my husband's childhood dogs, snapped Gracie's leash onto her collar, and opened the door, bracing myself for her to throw herself out on the front step and take off like a rocket.

Instead, she calmly stepped over the threshold and looked back at me, standing still until I pulled the door shut behind us.

"Let's go?" I suggested, and she complied, trotting down the steps ahead of me. We walked to the end of the driveway, hung a right and followed the sidewalk away from our townhome.

Sixty paces later, she froze, her eyes riveted on something in the ravine that ran behind our home. Her ears stood at attention, and her tail was curled tightly above her body in a perfect "o". The tension in her body flew right up the leash and into my arm and heart. I caught my breath, afraid to see a coyote or rabid raccoon come barreling out at us from the lightly leafed bushes that lined the ravine.

But nothing moved.

I followed the direction of Gracie's gaze just as a magnificent Great Blue Heron—almost completely camouflaged by the shadows of the trees—gracefully lifted up on its spread wings and slowly rose out of the ravine.

I caught my breath in wonder. I'd been watching birds for decades, but I'd never seen a Great Blue Heron up so close. Its feathers shimmered silver in the sunlight.

The bird sailed away, and Gracie continued to pull me down the sidewalk—not too fast and not too hard, but with a certain sense of mission. Another few yards and she attained her objective by liberally watering a small shrub along the edge of the ravine.

Still thinking about the heron—a heron that had probably roosted in those trees in the ravine every year, but which I'd never seen—I decided that walking the dog wasn't such a bad task after all. What else was in my backyard that I'd neglected to see because I'd been afraid to get out of my own home for a mid-day walk?

We strolled for forty-five minutes, Gracie in the lead as we wandered a nature trail behind our housing community. The sun was out, the air mild and fresh, the trail muddy.

By the time we got home, I was feeling pretty confident that I could walk a dog successfully, even if her feet were caked in mud and leaves.

"We've got to rinse those feet," I told her when we returned to our front walk. Tugging her along behind me, I grabbed the garden hose and turned on the faucet. Water shot out of the nozzle . . . and Gracie was gone.

Her collar, the leash still attached, lay on the grass.

Gee, I thought, *Gracie must be afraid of a hose.*

In the next split second, two thoughts popped simultaneously into my head. The first: Could this be my golden opportunity to worm my way out of the whole dog situation and tell my daughter and husband, "she ran away, I'm sorry"? And the other was: "This poor dog—did someone beat her with a hose?"

Before I had fully registered either thought, though, I was already sprinting around the corner of our home in the direction I'd caught a glimpse of her bolting. I ran to the edge of the ravine that backed up to our yard and frantically scanned the woods for a sign of Gracie. I heard some crashing in the bushes and spotted her at the bottom of the ravine, jumping over the small stream to land on the opposite side. I called her name and she looked up at me, her ears perked up and—if I didn't know better—what looked suspiciously like a big grin on her face.

"Gracie!" I called again. "Get back up here!"

Right . . . like that was really going to happen.

While I watched from the rim of the ravine, she turned and ambled along the stream, sniffing at leaf piles and pawing at sticks.

I was going to have to go get her if I wanted this dog to come home.

Did I want her to come home?

The thought that this was my path to a dog-free life again presented itself. Gracie had run away from me, it was true. I wouldn't be lying when I told my daughter and husband how the dog went missing.

But the idea that Gracie might have been abused in her past by someone with a hose tore at my heart. No animal deserved to be hurt by a human.

Especially one that now belonged to our household.

Shoot.

I was going to have to go get the dog.

I knew I had to climb down the hill, and that I would have to grab branches or bushes to make my way down the slope. I knew I'd have to be careful, so I wouldn't lose my footing in the muddy earth and go tumbling down to the stream. I was going to have to step where there might be snakes or spiders hiding. I might break my ankle or even my leg trying to bring the dog back.

"It doesn't matter," I told myself. "I have to get the dog . . . God help me."

I want to point out that I wasn't taking the Lord's name in vain when I said that, either. At that moment, I absolutely, completely, honestly asked God to help me, because I *knew*, without a doubt, that I couldn't retrieve the dog alone.

Do not fear, for I am with you.

The scripture rang in my head. I'd memorized the line from Isaiah 41:10 during my positive self-talk phase of trying to control my anxiety, but it had never seemed to hold my fears in check.

This time, though, it was different. I didn't have any other option. I had to trust that God would lead me down into the ravine and bring me back up again. I wasn't going to admit to my daughter that I—a grown woman, mother of five, college professor and author—couldn't muster the courage to go into the woods where the neighborhood children regularly played with abandon.

I made the leap of faith.

If you'd been watching at the time, however, my "leap" looked a lot more like a clumsy thrashing through the bushes than a grace-filled surrender to God.

Then again, this wasn't a finely choreographed movie moment, by any means. This was my backyard.

And so I plunged down the hillside, ignoring the sharp branches that scratched at me, the slippery ground that threatened to slide away beneath my feet, the hidden dangers lurking in the ravine. Heedless of every fear nagging at me, I made my way to Gracie, who was much too interested in sniffing a rotted tree to be concerned with my screaming legion of inner anxieties and the spiritual battle I was waging against them.

"Just stay right there," I told her as I approached, trying to sound as relaxed as if I made the treacherous trek down the ravine at least twice a day. "What a good girl you are," I added for extra measure.

She glanced at me, and in that moment, I reached out and slipped my left hand under her throat while my right hand dropped the collar over her neck and closed the clasp.

"You stinker," I said, relieved and a little—okay, a *lot*—surprised that she hadn't bolted again before I'd reached her. I turned and headed back up the slope with Gracie trotting obediently behind me.

Just as if we did this at least twice a day.

"We are not going to do this again," I sternly informed her. "Not even once."

Yet, I reflected as I climbed up to our backyard, it hadn't been nearly as impossible as I had first assumed. There weren't a hundred accidents or vicious animals waiting for me in the woods. Instead, there was the spring smell of the earth, the trickling sound of the stream, birds calling, buds opening. It was beautiful.

Thanks to Gracie, I'd experienced it all up close and personal.

Maybe a little too up close.

I surveyed a bloody scrape on my ankle that was beginning to sting and hoped I hadn't picked up deadly bacteria. I at least needed to get Gracie into the house before I died, or the whole diving into the ravine thing would be for naught. Then I idly wondered when the last time was that I'd come in with a scrape from an outdoor adventure.

For that matter, when had I last wandered off the sidewalk, let alone plunged into unknown territory?

"It's a whole new world," I told the dog, "being a dog owner."

Then I corrected myself.

"Or rather, it's a world I've been missing, isn't it, Gracie?"

I led her into the house, and she followed me as I went to grab some towels from the hallway linen closet. Muddy paw prints left a trail across our wood floors. No hose bath for this dog. I wet the towels and wiped her feet and flanks clean of the dirt.

Welcome to what would quickly become my world.

What I didn't know
at that moment was
that research studies
consistently show that
dog owners, as a whole,
are physically and
emotionally healthier than
their non~dog owning
counterparts.

Chapter 4

It would help if the dog read the books, too

My husband cannot help himself. Every night at the end of dinner, he offers Gracie a few tidbits from his plate. She has trained him well; throughout the meal, she lays on her blanket in the living room, only to walk over to wait by my husband's chair just as we're taking our last bites. He holds out to her a small piece of chicken or a chunk of biscuit, which she gently takes from his fingers and politely chews and swallows. She waits patiently for seconds.

"You're just encouraging the behavior," I remind him for the thousandth time.

"I know," he smiles ruefully. "But how can I resist that face and those big brown eyes?"

I sigh in resignation and shake my head. It would help if he'd read the stack of books about dog training and dog ownership that I'd devoured the first week of Gracie's residency with us.

But then again, Gracie hasn't read them, either.

Within a day of our ravine escapade, I had my hands on a pile of books from the local library. Being a teacher by profession, I have a lot of confidence in being able to learn almost anything if I set my mind to it. Gracie's reaction to the hose convinced me I needed a crash course in dog psychology if I was ever going to learn how to manage life with a canine family member. One of my older daughters is a huge fan of Cesar Millan, the Dog Whisperer, and she urged me to read his books to gain insight into Gracie's behavior. Not one to skim the surface of a subject, I cleaned out the library shelves of every book by Millan, along with every other dog owners' guide, in my quest to get inside my new dog's head and skin.

While it was educational, it wasn't always pretty.

Or palatable.

For instance, although I think it's totally disgusting to gobble up the remains of a cheeseburger that I might find in the gutter along the sidewalk, a dog—a scavenger by nature—will conclude it has found a gourmet delight. Likewise, my sensibilities are offended by seeing a pile of dog waste in a fresh drift of snow, but my dog may consider it a quick and very edible pickme-up. Neither of those inclinations is contrary to the nature of a dog, but simply an expression of *dogness.*

I may not like it, but there it is: dogs will eat almost ANYTHING.

All dog owners tell stories of the weird stuff their dogs have eaten: foam mattresses, stuffed toys, underwear, holiday ornaments, car dashboard hula dancers, drywall, softballs, and entire boxes of Girl Scout cookies. (Okay, I confess. I've eaten entire boxes of Girl Scout cookies, too, but I did *not* eat the cardboard packaging itself, unlike some dogs I could name.) The only reason we believe these are weird things to eat is because we humans make distinctions about what is edible and what is not. Distinctions are abstract ideas.

Dogs don't have abstract ideas.

Quite frankly, I'm not even sure if dogs have ideas. Based on everything I've read about dogs, it seems they live totally in the moment, responding to stimuli and eating it, or maybe just going back to sleep. Dogs don't wrestle with philosophical questions or the appropriateness of certain items going into their stomach. The Dog Whisperer claims that after a dog's basic survival requirements of shelter and food are met, the dog has three needs: exercise, discipline, and love. If you can give your dog those things, it will become a great pet. Raised on exercise, discipline, and love, your dog will be satisfied with life, provide you with companionship, and not eat the family cat or bird. (No guarantees about favorite socks or dead mice, however.)

The main idea here is to always make sure the dog is too tired to argue or do anything but follow you into your house at the end of the day and collapse. A happily exhausted and docile dog makes it much easier for you to revel in the joys of dog ownership.

So after reading through my stack of books as fast as I could, I determined I could be a pretty good dog owner if I followed the Dog Whisperer's advice. Since love was going to be a bit of a challenge for me—I had fifty-plus years of disliking and fearing dogs, remember—I decided that exercise and discipline would be my priorities for Gracie. Since my daughter was the one who had pleaded for a dog, we'd already agreed she would walk Gracie every day and take her to obedience classes at our local pet store. The dog was "her" dog, after all.

"Gracie needs ten miles of walking a day since she's a big dog and part Labrador Retriever," I told Colleen after reading my tomes of dog owner wisdom. "That should keep her happy, relaxed, and harmless."

My daughter looked at me like I was speaking an alien tongue. I don't mean Spanish, Russian, Chinese or Swahili, either. I mean really alien, as in Martian.

"Ten miles," Colleen finally echoed.

"Yes. Ten miles," I repeated. "I guess you're going to get that exercise you wanted."

"There is no way I can walk ten miles every day," she proceeded to argue. "For one, I don't have that kind of time since I'm in school all day. And when I get home, I have homework to do and piano to practice."

"You're saying you're not going to walk *your* dog?" I emphasized the possessive pronoun.

"No, no," she immediately insisted, clearly remembering her promises to care for the dog. "I just can't manage all ten miles a day, Mom. I need you to help me out. Can't you walk her in the afternoon if I walk her in the morning before I go to school and in the evening before I go to bed? If you can walk her once a day, I can do the other two times."

A tiny voice whispered inside my head.

It's the beginning of the end. She's not going to be able to take care of this dog. It's way more than she bargained for, which is no surprise, since none of you knew what you were getting into when it came to adopting a dog. You're an idiot, Jan. You're an idiot who is going to end up with a dog. A big dog that you have to spend the day walking. Your life, as you knew it, is over.

Some days, I really hate the tiny voice in my head.

Especially when it's right.

So instead of reminding Colleen once again that I wasn't the one who had begged for a dog, I kept my mouth shut. Out of fairness, I had to accept that my daughter was only sixteen years old. My tiny voice was right: how could Colleen possibly have appreciated the amount of work and time a big active dog would require when Tom and I, her older and supposedly wiser parents, had been equally clueless?

The bottom line was that I had agreed to the adoption, and that meant I had to take responsibility for my decisions.

Certainly, I could walk the dog once a day. I'd already done it several times by then, though I'd been very careful to avoid any hoses, and I'd cinched Gracie's collar up a notch to make sure she couldn't pull out of it.

And the daily walks I'd taken with Gracie while Colleen was at school were admittedly pleasant; it was spring in Minnesota, and the fresh air was heavenly after a long winter of being cooped up inside.

"I can do that," I assured her. "A daily walk is . . . nice."

Idiot, the tiny voice repeated.

I ignored it. Walking outside *was* nice, even though I still worried about keeling over from a sudden heart attack as Gracie increased our pace. She was a big dog, after all. And while she didn't exactly drag me along, I did have to keep up a brisk stride or she'd gradually work my left arm out of its socket. My consolation was that if I did fall over in dire distress on the sidewalk, someone would certainly notice a big black dog standing over a body and come to my rescue. Maybe she wasn't as portable as an emergency call button on a lanyard around my neck, but in a pinch, I figured Gracie could get the same results if necessary.

Not that I could tell her to run home and get help, mind you. She wasn't exactly Lassie, who would run home to get help every time Timmy fell into a well. But I had to admit I felt safe outside with Gracie. I figured she was noticeable enough that it was like carrying a sign every time I walked with her: DOG WITH PERSON ATTACHED. APPROACH WITH

CAUTION OR I WILL EAT YOU. AND IF SOMETHING IS WRONG WITH MY PERSON, PLEASE CALL 911.

And so the daily noon walk became our routine until the morning when Colleen did not get up early enough to walk the dog before her school bus arrived.

"Thanks, Mom!" my daughter called as she ran to catch her bus at the corner.

I walked the dog, and since it was a lovely spring morning, we wandered the neighborhoods along with the trails. Then I walked her again at noon, and we retraced our steps from earlier in the day. By the time Colleen got home from school that afternoon, I was draped across the living room sofa, exhausted and sure I'd walked Gracie's required ten miles.

Gracie, on the other hand, was a dancing ball of energy.

"Does she need to walk?" Colleen asked me. "She's acting like she wants to go out."

I glared at the dog.

"Ten miles!" I told Colleen. "I've walked ten miles with her today and she still wants to go out. The book said ten miles would do it. Ten miles would tire her out, make her mellow and happy."

"She clearly hasn't read the book," Colleen observed, "but she does look happy."

My daughter studied my face. "So do you, Mom."

She was right, I realized. I was happy —happier than I'd felt in a long time. I smiled at my daughter.

"I don't think I can take this much happiness," I commented with a laugh. "My feet are killing me."

What I didn't know at that moment was that research studies consistently show that dog owners, as a whole, are physically and emotionally healthier than their non-dog owning counterparts. In 1980, a study of survival rates of coronary care patients concluded that pet ownership contributed to longevity and that additional research should be conducted into the human-animal relationship in terms of health benefits; in particular, the question of whether the positive effect was due to physical activity with the pet or the pet-owner's psychological bond to the pet needed to be addressed.[1] Four years later, a team of researchers collected evidence that petting your own dog led to a decrease in blood pressure that equaled the relaxation achieved by quietly reading.[2]

One of the most obvious physical benefits of dog ownership, however, is increased exercise for the owner. In the last decade, dog walking has garnered the attention of fitness and medical professionals as a great way to lose weight and improve cardiovascular health. Titles like *Walk a Hound, Lose a Pound: How You and Your Dog Can Lose Weight, Stay Fit, and Have Fun Together,* authored by Phil Zeltzman, DVM, DACVS and Rebecca Johnson, PhD, RN, advocate dog walking as a way to ward off disease, and obesity in particular.

Johnson, the director of the Research Center for Human/ Animal Interaction (ReCHAI) at the University of Missouri College of Veterinary Medicine in Columbia, has studied human-animal interaction for more than a decade, and is an internationally known expert on the subject. Initially focused on research using therapy dogs to help the elderly adjust to lifestyle changes, Johnson quickly recognized that the results she witnessed were applicable to people of all ages. The original "Walk a Hound, Lose a Pound" program that she supervised in Columbia involved elderly participants walking shelter dogs for exercise as a way to improve their general health. Not only did the walkers enjoy better health in the course of the program, but their routine of dog walking also impressed them with the importance of getting more exercise on a regular basis.

Johnson's latest project teams combat veterans with shelter dogs in need of obedience training. The results benefit both the human and the dog participants: the training and increased socialization that the dogs receive make them more adoptable, while the veterans experience alleviation of post-traumatic stress disorder (PTSD) symptoms thanks to the bond they establish with their canine partners.

Clearly, dogs are good for your nerves as well as your body.

In the past few years, the neurological news about pet ownership has gotten even better. Recent studies have verified that humans' levels of the hormone oxytocin rise in the course of interacting with animals. That's a good thing, since oxytocin triggers feelings of trust and attachment, which correspond to decreased levels of emotional stress. Sometimes referred to as the "love hormone" because of its bonding influence between people, oxytocin's effects reach beyond emotional outcomes: studies show that it can reduce withdrawal symptoms from addictive substances; it lowers physical stress markers; inhaling it improves the social skills of autistic individuals; it promotes sleep; and it stimulates women's uterine contractions during the birth process and facilitates breast milk production.

(If I'd known all that years ago, I would have been petting a whole pack of dogs while I gave birth to my first child. Laboring for nearly twenty-four hours was not the most pleasant aspect of becoming a new parent, believe me.)

Even colleges are jumping on the "dogs are good for you" bandwagon. A room filled with puppies was available to students at Canada's Dalhousie University during finals week last December to help relieve student stress at the end of the term. Brought in by Therapeutic Claws of Canada, a volunteer organization providing animal resources for human needs, the puppies were such a hit with the students that news of the room went viral on Twitter. The non-profit organization reports that it has had a string of inquiries about providing a similar service for other colleges in the wake of the publicity.

ReCHAI's Johnson believes that oxytocin may also provide humans with longer-term health benefits. According to a research study at Israel's Weizmann Institute of Science, oxytocin is involved in embryonic brain cell formation.[3] Because of this neural connection, the hormone might be relevant to disease treatment, or as Johnson says, it "predisposes us to an environment in our own bodies where we can be healthier."

In an era of increased public concern about the prevalence and health dangers of obesity, the weight-loss effect of dog walking is nothing to walk away from. Combined with the physiological and neurological rewards of increased oxytocin, dog ownership might just be a prescription from which everyone could benefit. In my own case, I lost five pounds in the first six weeks of walking Gracie, not to mention all the fresh air I breathed and the pure pleasure I took in watching spring once again take a firm hold in winter-weary Minnesota. Yes, my feet were sore, but my spirit (and footfall!) was lighter than it had been in years.

One early morning, about a week after Gracie had come to live with us, she and I were close to finishing what was becoming our routine path around the edge of a neighboring golf course. As usual, I was running out of steam, while her enthusiasm continued to swell, mostly in the form of practically dragging me along.

"You're supposed to wind down after a long walk," I complained to her, "not speed up."

Again, I ruefully remembered my daughter's comment that Gracie hadn't read the books, so the fact that my plan to tire her out had not only failed, but had also been doomed from the start, simply added to my growing frustration that I couldn't make this dog do what I wanted. At that moment, we crossed paths with a couple from our townhome community who were also out enjoying the morning air.

"Who is this?" Judy, one of the two, asked as she offered her palm for Gracie to sniff.

Gracie stepped close to my side and delicately stretched her neck out to sniff Judy's hand.

"This is Gracie," I said, noting that when it came to meeting new people, our dog knew exactly how to put her best foot—or paw—forward. "We adopted her from a rescue group."

"Grace!" Judy exclaimed. "God's gift!"

Not if you'd seen me climbing down into that ravine, I silently objected, *or waking up every morning thinking that my days were now scheduled around a dog I didn't want. I'd hoped that God liked me better than to put me on perennial scoop-up-poop duty.*

"Yes," I finally agreed, not wanting to disappoint my neighbor nor offend her religious sensibilities. Her broad smile was filled with the happy expectation that I felt the presence of God in all things, including my dog. Unconvinced that our rescued lab mix was on a mission from The Big Guy, though, I hedged my final comment. "Grace is certainly a gift from God."

Note that I didn't specify a certain dog named Gracie that happened to be waiting next to me was a gift from God. I simply acknowledged what I knew from all my theological studies to be true: grace is God's free gift to humanity.

Yet as we continued on our way home, my neighbor's words struck a sudden chord in my heart.

Could Gracie be a special grace just for me?

I mulled over the past week. I hadn't asked for this dog, but it was, through no intention of my own, changing my life. I no longer hesitated to go for a walk around the neighborhood, and while I didn't feel invulnerable, I wasn't obsessing about being attacked or struck dead when I stepped outside. One reason was that I now had a dog to protect me—I felt physically safe, which seemed to reassure me emotionally, as well. I had been so preoccupied with trying to figure out how to manage the disaster of a dog in my home that I hadn't had time to think about anything else. I had forgotten to look for personal disaster around every corner.

Clearly, preoccupation with a dog was healthier for me than preoccupation with my health, and thanks to the dog walking, I felt physically better than I had in a long time. On top of that, my daughter had pointed out that I looked happy.

Most curious and surprising to me, though, was that I was no longer afraid of dogs. A fear I had lived with for half a century had disappeared in a matter of days, and my current slide into an anxiety disorder had come to a sudden halt.

Because of a dog.

It might not have been my plan to get my life back by taking Gracie into our family, but that was clearly what was happening to me.

Your Father knows exactly what you need, reads Matthew 6:8.

We stopped at the corner, waiting to cross the street. I looked at Gracie, who was now seated on her haunches beside me, big brown eyes gazing into my own, looking for all the world like an aspiring poster dog for adopting rescued animals.

Slap a phrase on her photo—personally, I like the one that goes "You had me at woof"— and she'd be a marketing sensation.

But to be God's own grace for *me*? A dog I had to walk, feed, and clean up after?

I knew that God worked in mysterious ways, but the idea that a dog could lead me into a renewed relationship with Him was a bit more of a stretch than I could manage. Seriously, how could a dog succeed where four years of theological study had failed?

And as for being a free gift of God, I only had to look at my checkbook to prove that point wrong, thanks to adoption fees, immunizations costs, and the price of a super-size bag of dog food.

Grace sure didn't come cheap these days.

I began to cross the street, but Gracie remained seated. I tugged on the leash.

She didn't budge.

Okay, I thought, *some days Grace doesn't come at all. Or at least, not when you want her to.*

Sometimes, though, I suddenly realized, you get revelation instead.

Chapter 5

Chasing Grace

The best thirty-five bucks I spend every year is the money I pay for our annual pass to the local dog park.

Managed by the regional park system, our dog park spreads out a full 27 fenced acres with a variety of terrain, including woods, rolling prairie, mowed play space, and even a pond that fills every spring when the snow melts. Almost every morning year-round, after my husband leaves for work, I grab Gracie's water jug, her leash, my ball cap (in winter, it's my face mask and woolen mittens), plastic bags, and the park pass. We hop in the car—Gracie, as always, sitting straight up in the back seat—and I drive the three miles to the park.

Depending on the day of the week, we meet the human and dog friends we've made at the park and set out to walk and run together. These dog owners have become some of my closest and best friends—people I never would have met without

Gracie in my life. We talk about everything: our dogs, our jobs, our spouses, favorite doggie day-care facilities, our kids, our health, split dew claws, books, travel destinations, fleas and ticks, chewing on slippers, and worms.

Fascinating conversation, I know. It's like a health club, in a way; you pay to use the dog park facility to exercise your dog, but one of the best benefits are the relationships you establish with the other people there. I never would have guessed that dog poop could be such a bonding experience.

Spending time at the park is also a great opportunity to practice multi-tasking. I watch where I walk so I don't step in a doggy dump that somebody failed to pick up; I watch Gracie so I can clean up where she takes her own doggy dumps; I step around ice patches in the winter and mud-holes in the spring; and I keep an eye on other dogs as they come bolting down the trail in pure joy, even while I'm discussing the merits of different dog diets with other walkers.

Knowing where the dogs are at all times is one of the most important skills I've learned since becoming a dog park regular: I'm not the only two-legged visitor who's been knocked over by an exuberant four-legged ball of energy. Dogs have an uncanny ability to not see unwieldy humans in their path while pursuing another dog—or better yet, a tossed ball.

Gracie, unlike many of her buddies, is not a ball-crazy dog. Whereas some dogs go absolutely nuts when their person pulls out a ball, Gracie can take it or leave it. Even when she is in the mood to chase a ball that I throw, the thrill seems to be gone once she picks it up in her mouth. She chews on it for a minute, then drops it and walks away. Forget about her bringing the ball back to me for another throw; if I'm so interested in throwing the ball, I have to go get it myself. Just a short while into Gracie's residence with us, I concluded that her Labrador Retriever retrieving instincts must have been diluted in the genetic stew of her lineage.

Not so with her instinct for couch-lounging; she's a world-class champion at that.

What Gracie does love at the park, though, is having another dog chase her when she's got a ball in her mouth. Then it's—literally—a whole new ballgame. If she has a canine pal tearing after her to try to gain possession of the ball, Gracie will play her heart out. She'll run like the wind, feint turns, and tease her playmate with an occasional drop of the ball, only to pick it up as her buddy closes in. Then she's off again like a shot. Every morning when we get in the car to go to the park, I feel like I'm a young mom again, headed for the playground with my children. Except now, once we arrive at the park the "kids" sniff each other's rear ends and wag their tails instead of wave hello.

I discovered the dog park in a moment of desperation about two weeks after we adopted Gracie. Remember that ten-mile-a-day walking goal I set?

It wasn't working.

At least, it wasn't working for Gracie.

I, on the other hand, was exhausted, and the dog still wanted to go out every hour of the day, whining and barking at me practically every time I sat down. I was falling behind in grading my online students' work because I could only get to their submitted assignments after Colleen came home from school and took over the dog walking. And while I'd never been a blue-ribbon housekeeper, the household chores were piling up into my own intolerance zone—I could write my name in the dust on the shelves, and my favorite jeans had spent a week at the bottom of the dirty clothes basket. Not only that, but in another two days, I was going to be the sole dog exerciser since Colleen was going on a school trip to New York City, and Tom's mobility was limited by a recurring case of plantar fasciitis which kept his feet in pain.

I had to find a way to tire out the dog.

Or, I firmly told myself, we couldn't keep her. Not because I wanted her gone—which I was no longer so sure of—but because we couldn't give her what she needed to be happy and healthy, namely sufficient exercise. Being the avid student I am, I'd taken to heart what I'd learned in my marathon reading about dogs. In particular, the Dog Whisperer's formula of exercise, discipline, and love had sunk deep into my consciousness.

In other words, I was obsessed with getting Gracie enough exercise.

"Why don't you take her to the off-leash dog park in Victoria?" Tom asked when I shared my frustration (and growing panic) with him. "She can run all she likes there."

"A dog park? With other dogs around?" It was true that I was no longer afraid of Gracie, but the idea of surrounding myself with other dogs— dogs I didn't know, dogs with their own teeth and bloodlust—was intimidating, to say the least.

"Jan," my husband said, "just give it a try. You want Gracie to get exercise? Take her to the dog park."

The afternoon my daughter left for New York, I opened the car door for Gracie to get in the back seat.

"This better work," I told the dog in the rear view mirror as I pulled out of our garage. "Or one of us is going to be house-hunting, and it's not going to be me."

To my relief, only a few cars were parked in the lot at the dog park. Recognizing that the chances were slim that I might be swarmed by a huge pack of uncontrollable dogs, I parked in the lot. While Gracie waited patiently in the car, I deposited the daily fee of five dollars into the designated box and put the permit on my front dashboard.

From inside the park, a dog barked.

Gracie's ears perked up, and she gazed intently through the car window at the latched gate to the park.

I attached her leash to her collar and opened the car door for her. Without any urging on my part, she trotted over to the gate. I pushed it open, she walked through, and I closed the gate behind her. As she waited in front of the second gate that would admit her to the playground beyond, I unsnapped her leash and opened the second gate.

She rushed inside and eagerly made a circuit of the gravel entrance area, sniffing loudly at every fencepost and shrub. Two dogs appeared on a path that led into the woods, and Gracie ran to greet them. After the ceremonial inspection that I would come to recognize as proper dog etiquette, Gracie came bounding back to me for a second before she returned to her sniffing. A few more dogs and owners showed up in the gravel area and everyone sniffed at will.

The dogs, I mean. Not the owners.

The dogs sniffed private areas. The owners said "hello."

Thank goodness.

"You should walk the trails around the park," a woman suggested. "Your dog can run and run, and you don't have to worry about her getting away from you, since it's all fenced."

"That would be nice," I admitted. I shared my story of Gracie's run into the ravine. "We've only had her with us for a couple of weeks, and I'm not sure that she wouldn't run away," I explained. "She was a stray when they first put her in a shelter, and she's been moved around a lot since then, we think."

I glanced at Gracie, who was done with her meet-and-greet with the other dogs. She was poised at the beginning of a path that led into the woods on one side of the park, her ears up, her tail curled, her nose lifted and lustily sniffing.

"Okay, Gracie," I told her as I walked over to join her. "Let's go!"

I didn't have to tell her twice. As soon as she saw me headed her way, she took off on the path. Within moments, I lost sight of her.

"Gracie!" I called.

To my complete surprise, she reappeared on the path ahead, racing back toward me.

I was stunned. She'd come at my call.

The dog slowed down, and when I got within ten feet of her, she turned around and headed back up the path. Again, I lost sight of her, and again, she came when I called.

In a straight stretch of the path, I watched her gallop away from me at full speed, then come to a stop and look back at me. I had the distinct impression that she was keeping tabs on me, that she wanted to be sure I was following her. I remembered the feeling I'd had the first few days with her—that I had become her security blanket.

Could she already be so attached to me that my presence was reassuring to her in a new and untested environment?

Did I look like a dog security blanket?

Granted, I'd certainly made great strides toward accepting her into our household, but as far as a real bond with her, I wasn't feeling it. She was still Colleen's dog in my mind, and I was her keeper, not her human. As far as I was concerned, my job was part one and two of the Dog Whisperer's three-part formula: providing the dog with the exercise and discipline she needed to be happy. Colleen's job was part three: supplying the love.

Gracie, meanwhile, investigated a small pond just off the trail. A preliminary sniff led to full immersion, which required Gracie to lay flat on her stomach and drag herself through the mud. A moment later, she leapt out and bounded away for more exploring.

I groaned and made a mental addendum to the three-part formula for dog health and happiness: exercise, discipline, love, and mud.

Lots of mud.

The next time I caught up with her, we had covered more than a third of the trail that circled the park. Gracie stood next to the five-foot-high wire fencing that separated the dog park from the surrounding wild area, peering into the depths of the woods on the other side. She panted a little, her pink tongue protruding over the edge of her front teeth.

"Good girl," I told her, patting her lightly on her head. "You're really getting a good run here, aren't you?"

Mentally, I pumped my fist in victory. I figured that today, with all the running back and forth she was doing, unleashed and unrestrained in any way, this dog was finally going to be tired out.

The dog park was the answer to Gracie's exercise needs. If we brought her here to run, she could get all the exercise she needed to be happy, healthy, and content in our home.

With a sigh of relief, I watched her speed down a hill, take a sharp turn and go sailing over the fence.

Out of the park.

"Gracie!" I yelled, running after her. "Come! COME!"

By the time I got to the section of fence she had jumped, she was long gone. I stared at the wire fence in disbelief. My dog had jumped out of the dog park.

My dog had cleared the fence.

Not knowing what else to do, I walked along the fence for fifteen yards in either direction, trying to catch a glimpse of Gracie.

Nothing.

I called her name.

Nothing.

Another dog and its owner approached me on the trail.

"My dog just jumped the fence," I told the young woman as she neared me.

It wasn't like I thought that this stranger could magically make Gracie reappear, but I felt like I had to say something as I stood there, a leash in my hand and no dog around. As an inexperienced dog handler, I was desperately hoping this was a typical thing that happened, and that this fellow dog owner might know an easy fix to the problem. For all I knew, maybe there was a readily accessible back gate through the fence that owners used to fetch their dogs when they jumped out of this side of the park.

"Are you serious?" she asked, a hint of awe in her voice.

Her tone made it clear I was wrong to hope—jumping the dog park's five-foot fence wasn't a common occurrence.

"And I've been calling for her," I added, not wanting her to think me irresponsible in addition to being inexperienced, "but she hasn't come back."

Okay, perhaps somewhere deep inside I hoped this young woman could somehow make Gracie reappear. After all, her Golden Retriever was standing quietly next to her, obedient and calm; surely she knew the trick to getting a dog to come.

"Wow," the woman said. "I hope you find her."

She walked away, her dog close to her side.

I heard a rustling in the branches beyond the fence and turned to look. Gracie thrust her happy face, tongue lolling out the side, up against the fence.

"What are you doing?" I asked her frantically. "Get back over here!"

She gave me a toothy grin and promptly took off again.

"Gracie! GRACIE!"

After another five minutes of walking and calling along the fence with no sign of a runaway dog, I gave up trying to find a way over the fence to continue the search on the other side. I would have to go back to the front gate, and follow the fence around the outside perimeter of the park, all 27 acres of it, and hope against hope that I would find Gracie.

And if I didn't?

I would have to tell Colleen that I had lost her dog.

Oh, yeah. That was going to be fun.

More like horrible.

Maybe I could find another black lab mix before she got back from New York. We'd only had Gracie for a few weeks; could Colleen even tell the difference?

I gave myself a mental head slap. What was I thinking? Of course she would be able to tell the difference. This was her dog. The dog she'd begged for; the dog that slept next to her bed every night. I had to find THIS dog, and I had to find it now.

I walked back to the gravel area and told the four people who were visiting there with their dogs what had happened.

"She jumped the fence?" an older fellow asked incredulously. "I've never heard of that happening here."

Again, not what I wanted to hear. I didn't know if I should be proud of Gracie, or even more upset. On the upside, my dog was clearly a gifted athlete if no other dog had been able to jump the five-foot high fence. It was sort of like having your kid win the pole-vault event at the school track meet. On the down side, though, my dog had wanted to run away from me so badly that she had jumped a five-foot high fence that no other dog had jumped. That was like getting a report card with a big F in the dog-owning column.

Unfortunately, either way I looked at it, it still meant the dog was AWOL.

"I'm going out to walk the perimeter," I told the other dog owners. "If you see a black lab mix with a purple collar and no person, would you please grab her? I'll come back here after I walk the park fence line. Her name is Gracie."

They readily agreed to grab my errant mutt should she appear. I headed out of the park and finally decided to call Tom and apprise him of the situation. I wondered briefly what he would think—he knew I wasn't crazy about having adopted a dog, and my history with Gracie so far had been less than awe-inspiring.

"Well, that's one way to get rid of her," he commented after I told him my story.

"Tom! I didn't do this on purpose!"

He chuckled into the phone. "I know you didn't. I'll come out and help you look."

"Are you sure? I know your feet are really hurting."

"I'll be there as soon as I can."

I ended the call, feeling a little less alone. My husband would make everything all right. He'd help me chase down the dog. I didn't know how he would pull that off, since a snail was probably faster at the moment than he was, but I had no doubt that everything was going to be all right.

For a little extra assurance, I prayed. "Just help me find the doggone dog, Lord."

I headed off into the tangled woods along the dog park fence, calling for Gracie and scanning the area.

"I can't believe I'm doing this," I muttered, picking my way carefully around spongy mounds of leaves and decaying forest matter. The air was thick with the smell of damp earth and rotting vegetation, the ground slippery and uneven. When my feet hit a patch of mud, I clung to the fence to keep myself upright. I wondered vaguely if wood ticks were out yet, because I knew that if they were, they were just waiting to latch onto my clothes.

Yes, I thought, *this is exactly what I wanted to be doing today—slogging through mud and collecting ticks.*

Ten minutes later, I'd barely made it halfway to where Gracie had jumped the fence. There was no sign of her anywhere. I tried to do some quick math in my head to estimate how far she could run in ten to twenty minutes.

Your dog jumps the fence out of the dog park at Point A and runs off at a speed of ten miles an hour due north. You, meanwhile, start at Point B outside the park and trace the perimeter of the fence around the park's 27-acres at one mile per hour. When will your paths intersect at Point C and/or how far will the dog get by the time the train arrives in Kalamazoo?

All right, I admit it. Solving story problems in math was never my strong suit. I was always more interested in why you'd name a town Kalamazoo than how long it took the train to get there. Throw in a dog, and I was totally lost.

I decided that locating Gracie through mathematical calculation was obviously not going to work. Since I had no idea where Gracie had gone, how fast she could run, or even if she had the vaguest notion that she was even lost, I decided my effort was wasted unless there were at least two of us searching for her. For all I knew, she may have been up ahead of me, following the fence in the same direction and at the same pace as I was, which meant we could be circling the park for all eternity. I needed Tom to help me walk a pattern in hopes we could find her.

I turned around and made my way back to the park's front gate.

As I walked, I rehearsed what I was going to tell Colleen when she got home if we couldn't find Gracie.

"We couldn't find her," I'd say. "We looked and looked, but she ran away. She was just too much to handle, I guess. Maybe she just wasn't meant for us. I'm so sorry."

Oh, yes. That would be a perfectly adequate explanation for how I'd lost her dog, when the truth was that I'd been an overconfident idiot who thought she could manage a strong-willed, active, untrained dog in a strange environment. As I approached the park's gate, I convinced myself that losing Gracie was probably inevitable. She was a high-energy dog who'd been abused and neglected and left to fend for herself almost since birth. She was used to being on her own; she knew how to survive without human help.

I sincerely hoped she would be happy.

And safe.

And fed.

Like that always happens for stray dogs.

Shoot. I had to find Gracie. She'd already done her time as a stray, and I wasn't going to let it happen again.

As I neared the gate, I could see the same knot of people and dogs by the picnic tables in the gravel area inside the park. When I opened the inner gate door, one big black dog detached itself from the crowd and made a beeline directly for me.

It was Gracie.

With her tail sweeping wildly from side to side, her teeth lining a big smile, and her tongue hanging out the side of her mouth, she locked her eyes on mine. She danced around me, joy radiating from her like a physical wave that washed over me. She stopped in front of me and stretched her nose up to sniff at my belly.

"Is that the dog you were missing?" called one of the women at the picnic table.

"Yes," I called back in shock. "This is Gracie."

"She obviously jumped the fence back into the park to find you," the woman added.

I looked down into Gracie's glowing brown eyes, and all I could think of was the song lyric we sing in church based on Psalm 139: "Where can I run from Your love? If I climb to the heavens You are there; If I fly to the sunrise or sail beyond the sea, still I'd find You there."[4]

There was no way I was going to lose this dog, I realized, and not because I was an excellent dog owner. I was not going to lose

Gracie, because she wouldn't let me.

Is that how God loved me?

The question popped into my head, and the answer followed right behind: no matter how far I strayed, I would never lose Him, because He wouldn't let me. He was always there.

That revelation was immediately followed by another as the words of the shelter volunteer came back to me in a flash of understanding: "She'll jump a fence to get to you."

I just hadn't picked up on the unspoken corollary: the dog somehow had to get on the other side of the fence first.

I totally got that part now.

"She must really love you," the man at the picnic table observed, "to jump back into the park."

I looked at Gracie's happy face.

"Yes," I said, still stunned by her voluntary reappearance. "I guess she really must."

The strength of the dog-human bond is no surprise to those who have studied the evolution of our canine companions. In her book *Made for Each Other: The Biology of the Human-Animal Bond,* Meg Daley Olmert traces the historical development of our relationship with dogs from the earliest wolf bones found in human settlements to today's working partnerships of canines and people. Working from archeological evidence, researchers have suggested that as humans formed small communities to ensure safety and survival, an increased emphasis on caring for our young physiologically stimulated the increased production of the hormone oxytocin in individuals. Given that oxytocin generates higher levels of trust and attachment, Olmert speculates that the human fascination with animals, coupled with their burgeoning nurturing instinct, led to human contact with those wolves brave enough to penetrate early campsites in search of food. As these first forerunners of our pets in turn learned to trust their human neighbors, Olmert explains, we forged an alliance that benefited both sides: dogs helped men hunt and offered increased protection from other predators, and in return, the dogs were fed and sheltered.

This alliance was a very early example of "you scratch my back, and I'll scratch yours." Or more like, "you feed me on a regular basis, and I'll tear apart anything that threatens you." Good puppy.

Modern research reveals, however, that the improvement of survival odds probably wasn't the only benefit the first dogs enjoyed from hanging around their human companions. In contemporary studies of human-canine relationships, the level of oxytocin in dogs likewise rises during pleasurable interactions with humans. In one study, the measure of blood levels of oxytocin in *both* the dogs and owners nearly doubled.[5] Given that oxytocin triggers feelings of attachment and nurturing in mammals, this mutual feedback loop may have been instrumental in allowing early humans and dogs to approach each other with increased confidence. Olmert calls it a "biological synergy" that enabled the two species to "form the friendships that endure to this day."[6]

True friendships, however, reach beyond physiological, emotional, and biological boundaries. Friendships address the spirit, the very essence of an individual. The more time and effort I put into trying to understand and provide for Gracie, the more I felt like my relationship with her was, indeed, based on *friend*ship, rather than *owner*ship.

Could I be developing a spiritual bond with a dog?

As living creations of the same Creator, Gracie and I shared a Maker. Didn't that already put us in relationship to each other? Could He have sent me a fellow creature—an inarticulate one, this dog—to help me experience a faith that went beyond words and, instead, went straight to the heart?

Even when my own faith in God's providence for me had stumbled in the wake of my growing anxiety issues, I never doubted that God made all things work ultimately for my good, even if I couldn't see it at the time.

I just wasn't excited about His definition of "good."

I also believed that He'd given me my personal gifts, and, in particular, my mind, to know Him. Now I began to wonder if my spiritual failing in the area of total trust was the result of simple, foolish, human pride. Had I unwittingly cut myself off from the intimate experience of God that I craved, because I thought it was better to know Him on intellectual terms instead?

Was my head keeping my heart at bay?

At the dog park, I'd tried chasing Grace and come up empty. Just like when I tried to possess God through knowledge alone, I still came up short.

But when I gave up the chase and gave it to God, the dog was waiting for me.

Grace was waiting for me.

And so was God.

I just needed to jump back over the fence I'd blindly put up around myself. Better yet, I needed to tear the thing down.

So far in my
relationship
with our dog,
I hadn't driven
the train once.
Gracie was
the engineer, and
I was just along
for the ride.

Chapter 6

I get by with a little help
from my trainer

*I*t's time for my annual health check up, and as usual,
I dread having my vitals taken.

Not because I feel bad or ill—because actually, I feel quite
healthy—but because I'm always disappointed with the results.
Chalk it up to my competitive nature, but I want my numbers
to land in the 'excellent' range, not the 'good' section.

Gee, maybe 'competitive' isn't the right word here. Can you
say 'overachiever'?

Actually, you can probably add 'obsessive' to that. Ever
since my false-positive stress test experience, I exert more than
due diligence in trying to improve my health, while still being
mindful that ultimately, it's God's call about my earthly longevity. At the same time, though, if I learned nothing else from my
heart scare, I came away convinced that an ounce of prevention
is worth a lot more than a pound of cure.

According to a multitude of medical studies, the right type of preventative care could even save your life. Let's face it—fish oil may not be the most delectable supplement to add to your diet, but if a world-class health clinic says it can significantly reduce the risk of heart disease, I'm excited to choke down those horse-sized pills every day.

Besides, if God didn't think exercise and a healthy diet were good things, He wouldn't have let anyone invent treadmills or put tofu in a recipe. Use it or lose it, right? It's biblical—God provides good stuff for us to use, and it's our job to be good stewards of it, whether it's time, talent, treasure or health. It's the idea behind the Parable of the Talents in Matthew 25:14-30, but think tofu and treadmills instead of coins.

Anyway, I'm scheduled for the annual exam today, so I take Gracie out for an early walk to accommodate my 8 a.m. appointment.

"How are you doing today?" the nurse asks as we walk back to the doctor's examining room.

"Great," I tell her. I step on the scale she indicates and watch the needle settle over the numbers.

"You've lost weight," she says as she scribbles the numbers on her clipboard.

No surprise there. I walk Gracie for two to three hours a day. The first summer after we adopted her, I lost two pant sizes, in fact. By August, I could have been an extra for a rapper's music video since my shorts kept falling down my hips.

We go into the exam room, and she positions the pressure cuff on my arm above my elbow. I watch the cuff inflate, then slowly return to its normal size.

"Excellent," the nurse says.

"What did you say?" I want to hear it again, just to be sure I wasn't imagining it.

"Your blood pressure is excellent," she says.

I do a fist-pump in my head.

She places her fingers on my pulse.

I quit the mental fist-pumping and breathe gently in and out. I will my pulse rate to slow.

She removes her fingers and enters the data into my online chart.

"Sixty beats per minute," she says. "That's excellent, too."

I almost jump off my chair and do a victory dance. Two "excellents" in one visit!

"Your numbers are the best they've ever been," the nurse comments as she closes out my chart. "What have you been doing?"

"I have a dog that I walk a lot," I answer. "She's my personal trainer. All winter long, every time it was sub-zero, I just kept telling myself, 'Other people go to a gym to work with their trainer. I'm lucky. My trainer is my dog. I don't have to go to the gym. I just have to walk outside . . . into subzero weather . . . several times a day. Thank you, Gracie.' Not that it made it any easier to go outside, but at least that way, I felt like I personally got something out of it beyond a doggie bag to carry back home."

"Well, I have a dog, too," she says, "but it's a chore to walk him because he's so stubborn. He either won't budge or he pulls too hard."

"I had the same problem with our dog before she went to doggy boot camp," I tell her. "It got so bad, I had to call my daughter to come pick us up with the car because I couldn't get the dog to move."

The nurse laughs.

"Yeah," I say, "it's funny now, but believe me, it wasn't at the time."

I desperately hoped no one was watching my pathetic attempts to be a masterful dog owner. It was a perfect early summer morning—bright blue skies, tank-top weather—and I was standing on a corner two blocks from our home. Gracie was sitting next to me on the sidewalk.

"Up!" I said, tugging upward on her leash.

Gracie didn't budge. The collar slid up under her ears, but she didn't bat an eye.

"Gracie! Up!" I tried again, throwing as much authority as I could muster into my voice.

We had taken a leisurely walk around the neighborhood, Gracie sniffing at will and wherever she pleased since I wasn't in a rush to go anywhere. But now, a full hour had passed. I needed to get home to use the bathroom myself, which clearly

didn't concern Gracie at all. Her bladder was comfortably empty after availing herself of the myriad opportunities for an outdoor toilet.

Me, not so much.

But how in the world did you get a 70-pound dog to walk
home when she didn't want to?

To be fair, it wasn't the first time our walk in the neighborhood had gone badly. About once a day, she was stubborn
at the end of her leash, planting her big paws and refusing to
come into the house, or even our yard, after a walk around the
block. Yes, I understood that dogs liked to be outside, but since
our townhouse didn't have a private yard, we had no choice:
Gracie couldn't spend her days lolling in the fresh air secured
by an electric fence. Our alternative was frequent walks, which
were generally pleasant until we got close to the house and she
balked at going in. So far, though, I'd always managed to cajole
her inside with the promise of a treat, even if sometimes the
progress she made was in increments of only a few feet at a
time.

It was like playing Monopoly with only one die, and drawing a "lose your turn" or "go to jail" card every other toss. But
instead of skipping a tiny little ship, shoe or top hat around the
board, I was pulling a dog that had turned into a one-ton block
of granite.

When it got to the point of requiring six doggy biscuits
alone just to get her up the driveway—let alone through the

front door—I decided the food incentive scheme was probably a mistake. I began to have visions of myself carrying ten-pound bags of peanut butter biscuits every time I stepped outside with her. I'm all for weight training, but 70 pounds of resistance at the end of a leash was not in my exercise plan.

On this particular morning, I'd already used up the supply of treats stashed in my pocket, which I belatedly realized was a fatal strategic error. As I continued to silently berate myself for underestimating my canine-commanding powers, several cars passed by with neighbors at the wheels.

I smiled and waved as if I had nothing else on my mind other than the lovely morning. Gracie looked up at me, confident she had the upper hand—or paw—in this particular situation. She had to know there was no way I could carry her the two blocks back home even if I was desperate.

"This is why people get little dogs," I warned her. "They can carry them home. They don't have to worry about cooperation because they can always control the situation. And right now, I have to say, a little dog sounds pretty good to me. So you'd better get up and start walking right now."

I gave her my sternest look.

She looked away.

I could tell she was reviewing her options. Or maybe she'd caught sight of a squirrel.

It's hard to tell for sure with dogs.

"Gracie," I growled at her.

She slowly stretched out her front legs . . . and laid down on the sidewalk.

"That's it! That's IT!" I ranted at her. "You have to get trained! I can't do this anymore! I can't have a dog I can't even walk back home!"

I pulled out my cell phone and called my daughter.

"I need you to get up and drive over here," I tersely told her. "I can't get Gracie to come home."

"What time is it?" she groggily asked.

"It's eight a.m.," I said.

"It's a Saturday morning," she pointed out.

"I know that, but the dog doesn't!" I almost shouted. "And dad's not answering his cell phone." Another car drove by. I enthusiastically waved and smiled.

"Just get over here," I snarled into the phone.

My intention was not for my daughter to take my place walking—or trying to walk—the dog, although I briefly considered it. I called my daughter-still-abed because there was one foolproof way to get Gracie home: in the car. Gracie loved the car. In the month or so that we'd had her, Gracie had never turned down the offer of a car ride. Every morning, in fact, she posted herself next to the house door leading to the garage in hopes someone would take her for a ride. It generally took a wrestling match to get into the garage without her, and when one of us humans lost, it took many dog treats to get her back into the house.

I wish we'd bought stock in some start-up dog treat company. At this rate, we were going to single-handedly—*pawed-ly*—make them millionaires in the years to come.

About three minutes later, my daughter drove up in the car and braked at the corner. Gracie immediately stood up, tail wagging with joy, and leapt toward the back passenger car door. I opened it for her, and she hopped up onto the seat, ears erect and mouth slightly open in her happy smile.

I climbed into the front passenger seat.

"I can't do this anymore," I said through gritted teeth. "I can't walk a dog that won't walk home. She has to go for training. Real training."

I looked over at my daughter. She was still in her pajamas.

"Do you have trouble getting her to walk home?" I challenged.

"Not really," she said as she turned the car around. "Gracie walks pretty well with me. I take her to the obedience classes, so that probably helps."

One of my original conditions for adopting Gracie was that Colleen would take full responsibility for taking her to weekly basic obedience classes at our nearby pet store, which she had faithfully done. After each class, Colleen then instructed me what to do with Gracie, so that we would be using the same commands and techniques as we developed our new dog-interaction routines. Yet it seemed that Gracie always performed better under the watchful eye of the store's dog trainer.

Colleen had no trouble with Gracie at the store, whereas at home, it often took her more effort to achieve the same results.

"I think Gracie is a little afraid of the trainer at the store, so she makes sure she keeps focused when we're there and does everything right," Colleen had noted one night after returning home from class. "When we're at the store, Gracie's the perfect student—she's the first one to heel, the first one to come, and she sits before I even get the word out of my mouth. Either that, or our dog is overly competitive," she added, "like everyone else in this family."

I'd heard rumors that dogs could pick up their masters' traits, but that would be ridiculous: our dog, the uber-competitor.

Wouldn't it?

"Mom," Colleen gently suggested as we drove the two blocks home, "you just have to let her know you're the boss."

Right. I'd been failing miserably at that since the day she came home with us from the adoption event—I'd been certain she was going to attack and eat me when she came into my room and rolled on her back, and I had screamed like a girl.

Even though none of that actually happened.

I mean the attacking and eating part.

The screaming like a girl part—that happened.

Then the dog had followed me all around the house like a stalker. Then I lost her in the ravine. Don't even mention the escape from the park. So far in my relationship with our dog,

I hadn't driven the train once. Gracie was the engineer, and I was just along for the ride.

And, I had to admit, she'd probably done a better job driving, because she'd both survived my incompetence and single-pawedly helped me overcome some big pieces of my anxiety issues. I was no longer afraid to go outside and wander the trails in our neighborhood, and I wasn't constantly afraid I was going to fall over dead, because I was too busy keeping an eye on the dog. Gracie had done for me what no amount of rationalizing or positive self-talk could do, and because of that, I had no doubt that God, in His great wisdom, had brought Gracie to me as my personal spiritual mentor.

More like a personal spiritual drill sergeant, really.

All I needed now was for her to let me walk her back home.

"I'm lousy at this," I finally admitted. "I need help. The obedience training you're doing with her isn't enough. I want her to go to doggy boot camp."

"Trainability," or more accurately, a *lack* of *training*, is a common reason for many adopted dogs' return to a shelter or rescue group, according to author McCuddy. In fact, misbehavior is most frequently the reason a dog lands in a shelter in the first place: when cute puppy antics become destructive or overwhelming behaviors, owners who don't take the time to train their pets, give them up instead. For some owners, incessant barking or manic responses to thunderstorms might even be intolerable, leaving the dog at risk of abandonment or surrender to a shelter. According to the American Veterinary Society of Animal Behavior, behavioral issues are the leading cause of death for dogs under the age of three years, and the greatest obstacle to forming lasting dog-human bonds.[7]

The behavioral outlook for rescued dogs can be even more complicated. Rescued dogs have a higher probability of having suffered physical or emotional injury in their lives prior to adoption, which could then surface as difficult behavior. When I took Gracie for her first medical checkup a few days after we'd adopted her, our veterinarian cautioned me that a rescued dog could take several months to exhibit behavior problems because the dog was stressed by the strangeness of its new situation.

"They stay on their best behavior when they first come to a new home," he explained. "It's like a defense mechanism. Once they relax, though—and it could be three or four months down the road—then you see the problem behaviors."

I was less than thrilled to hear it, to say the least. If my vet was correct, I could spend months learning to be comfortable around the dog, only to have her suddenly go psycho on me after I finally learned to trust her. Would I wake up one morning three months from now to find the house wrecked and the dog foaming at the mouth? Would I have to barricade myself in my bathroom and call the animal control hotline for a SWAT team?

(Except that I don't have a phone in my bathroom. Should I seek shelter there, it might be a long wait. I made a mental note to carry my cell phone at all times around the dog in case I needed to call for help in the event of her transformation into a rabid killing machine. I also made sure to keep a supply of reading materials on top of the toilet tank in case I found myself stuck in there with a whole lot of free time. I'm happy to report that two years later, Gracie still hasn't gone bananas, but I am now able to stay current with all my magazine subscriptions.)

"I'm just saying you need to give her time," my vet said. "With a rescued dog, you just don't know what kind of experiences she's had that may come back to haunt her."

Deciding that caution was the better part of rescued dog ownership, I resolved to keep my emotional distance from Gracie for the first few months. I already knew that keeping a physical distance from her was going to be impossible; I'd tossed that idea the first time she shadowed me from room to room in the house. And while it may be true that familiarity can breed contempt, it can also cement a habit: I didn't want to become attached to a pet that we'd have to give up either because she barked non-stop or ate through the walls of our home.

Of course, the emotional restraint strategy barely lasted a week. Call it inexperience or sheer stupidity, but I had no idea how quickly a big-eyed dog could suck in a soft human heart, especially when the soft human heart in question was mine. Once I realized that complete detachment from Gracie was not an option, I decided that behavioral psychology in the form of positive reinforcement was going to be our *modus operandi* for dealing with doggy issues. Positive reinforcement had gotten me through toilet training my five children, so I was optimistic that I could apply the same principles to Gracie.

I'd just have to stock dog treats instead of M&Ms if she decided to shred our furniture or water the rug.

Lots of dog treats.

Like I already said, I was going to make the dog treat company very rich.

We knew from the start that food as reward would be a successful training technique for Gracie, since the adoption volunteer had informed us that Gracie would do anything for food. Colleen also reported that at their pet store obedience classes, Gracie's focus on sitting, standing, and laying down to get her bacon-flavored treat was the envy of all the other dogs and their owners. The problem I couldn't seem to surmount was what happened when Gracie wasn't interested in what I wanted her to do . . . like walk home. I'd already tried all of the tips I'd picked up in my first wave of dog owner reading: be the leader of the pack (the alpha dog, in other words); be consistent with discipline; correct inappropriate behavior immediately; and understand how dogs experience the world so you won't expect them to act like humans.

Yet I still found myself losing our battle of wills at the ends of our walks . . . and having to call Colleen for a ride home.

To be honest, beginning to get a grip on animal psychology was probably the most helpful thing of all my early attempts to be a responsible dog owner. All the books and manuals and web articles I read gave me a clear understanding of how dogs are not human, and never will be, no matter how many cute Halloween costumes you make them wear. Dogs don't think like people. Dogs are all about their noses. They have between 25 and 60 times as many scent receptors in their noses as humans. We're talking about *at least 125 million receptors* here; using her nose is how a dog accesses the world.

Not only that, but a dog's brain is designed to efficiently process this overload of scent—a dog's olfactory brain cells outnumber a human's by 40 to 1. If you and I had those kinds of brain reserves dedicated to the sense of smell, we'd probably be rubbing our noses into everything and everyone we met, too. Why bother with polite, time-consuming introductions, when we could just sniff . . . uh . . . certain body parts . . . to learn if a new acquaintance might be friend or foe? Think about it—smells don't lie. There's no way you'll ever mistake a fresh orange for a rotten egg.

Understanding that Gracie was simply following her natural instincts when she sniffed her way around our neighborhood did reduce the impatience I initially felt with our drawn-out excursions. I even began to follow her lead, paying closer attention to the smells in the air as I slowly let go of using time as the measure for our walks. I watched the trees bud and flower and leaf out. I listened to the songs of the birds and finally learned to accurately identify which calls belonged to which birds. Our walks became a welcome time-out for me, a short respite from my daily routine of writing and teaching online.

Until we headed home. Then the stress came roaring in as I wondered if, once again, I would have to try to drag the dog the last few blocks.

As I became more frustrated with her, I researched training options beyond the basic obedience classes and decided that if I could not teach the dog to walk home, Gracie would spend three weeks at a training facility outside the Twin Cities. It would mean she would be trained with an electronic collar to obey our commands. And that was exactly why I resisted the plan for the first three months she lived with us: I considered a shock collar inhumane.

I wasn't unique in that respect. Many people reject formal training involving such collars for their dogs because they think it's cruel and fear it will damage the dog's natural personality. Yet there is a huge difference between training and animal abuse, and in some cases, you could argue that withholding necessary training is itself a form of animal abuse. When an untrained dog runs into the street and is struck and killed by a car, where does the blame lay? We teach our children not to run into a street filled with cars because we want them to have the tools of survival; isn't it also the task of a responsible dog owner to provide a pet with similar survival skills? Training a dog to comply with its owner's commands is a gift that may not only save the dog's life in a dangerous situation, but can also enhance the dog-human relationship itself as each party in that relationship comes to a point of mutual trust and understanding. Training is, ultimately, about communication. Without it, like any relationship, the dog-human bond suffers and both dog and human miss out on the full richness of their inter-species connection.

In our case, I finally accepted that the necessity of training Gracie to obey was crucial to our having a future together—a future I now wanted very much. In the three months she'd been living with us, I'd experienced a dramatic decrease in my stress levels and anxiety issues, and I felt a contentment in my life that had been missing since my heart scare four years earlier. Against all odds and everyone's expectations, I'd grown to love our dog, and there was no way I was going to give her up if there was a way I could keep her. Gracie was God's gift to me.

A stubborn gift, but a gift, nonetheless.

And so I registered Gracie for three weeks at Wings & Whistles, a training and boarding kennel not too far from our home.

"Train up a child in the way he should go," says Proverbs 22:6.

Okay, I knew Gracie wasn't a child. She was a dog. She'd always be a dog.

But with training, she might just become an obedient dog.

And 70 pounds of obedience absolutely sounded like a gift to me . . . even if I was going to have to write a fat check to pay for it.

What was it
going to take
to feel truly united
with God?
Why couldn't
I just
think myself
closer to God?

Chapter 7

Leaps of faith

After five months of snow and bone-numbing cold, the nighttime temperatures finally remain above freezing long enough to thaw our frozen lakes and streams. I throw an extra towel in the back seat of the car, and Gracie and I head for the dog park. I roll down her window just enough for her to stick her nose out. She enthusiastically inhales all the tantalizing hints of spring that fill the air, and her loud snuffling continues all the way to the park. Once we're out of the car, I take the path that leads toward the woods, while Gracie bounds around me like a springing deer.

Within a minute, I hear the first crash of water as she leaps into the vernal pond that fills with snow melt at the edge of the woods. By the time I catch up with her, she's doing her porpoise imitation across the surface of the pond, her sleek black body arcing up and down as she leaps wildly in the fresh, cold water, her coat shining with wetness.

"Your dog really likes the water," another dog-walker comments as he approaches.

"No," I correct him. "She *loves* the water."

"Trixie!" he calls to his dog, a mid-size retriever who is eyeing Gracie's performance, quivering with indecision about joining her in the icy wash. "No! Come."

Trixie turns away from the pond's edge and joins her master. I think she looks disappointed.

"It's too cold for you," Trixie's master tells her. I see her ears droop back.

He looks again at Gracie, who at this point is dragging herself through the shallows by her front legs, scooping up mouthfuls of water and tossing her head to clear her eyes from the splashing. "You should get her a wading pool for the summer," he says.

"Been there, done that," I tell him, thinking of the pool that now hangs from a hook in our garage. "She only likes natural bodies of water."

And mud holes, I mentally add, thinking ahead to spring. Gracie loves wallowing in mud. Sometimes, she even eats mud.

She is a dog, you know.

Finally sated, Gracie stands up in the pond, shakes off water, and comes bounding in my direction. Trixie and her master leave before she can get too close to shower them with cold droplets, but I welcome Gracie's exuberant embrace of the first open water as our private celebration of the return of spring.

"Behold, I make all things new," Christ says in the Book of Revelation 21:5.

I smile. The world is new all the time for me when I walk with Grace.

Moments like these are some of the greatest gifts my dog gives me on a daily basis: being totally in the present. Gracie's enthusiasm and openness to whatever comes her way models for me how to live in the moment, to open all my senses to *now*, and rejoice in pure being. Sometimes I think that the single most important thing Gracie teaches me is to get out of my head all the time—to stop imposing mental processing on every little thing that happens to me.

This proclivity to overthink, it turns out, is a common one in contemporary culture. Termed "rumination" by psychological researchers, it's defined as obsessive dwelling on a cause of personal distress. For many people, it takes the form of excessive self-reflection and a focus on negative thoughts stemming from a past bad experience or an anticipated future one. At its worst, rumination can lead to severe depression and frequently is associated with anxiety, bingeing, and self-harming behaviors.[8] In short, it's a bad habit that can jeopardize your health and destroy your happiness.

And guess what? Women are more prone to rumination than men.

Why am I not surprised? We're also more prone to depression, osteoporosis, migraines, knee injuries, self-criticism, PMS, and bearing children. All of which lead to anxiety, I might add.

Especially the bearing children part.

Speaking from my personal experience with anxiety, I'd say I'm an overthinking overachiever. Without a doubt, I almost ruminated myself into emotional paralysis after my heart scare. By constantly replaying in my head the whole episode from emergency room to angiogram and focusing on the unknowable and frightening causes of my false alarm, I guaranteed that I would feel increasing anxiety about my health. Having always trusted in my own ability to find answers if I just thought about a problem long enough, I had no resources to fall back on when the questions were unanswerable. For the first time in my life, my brain's mental processes couldn't offer me the comfort I sought, and even God seemed mute.

"Whatever overcomes a man, to that he is enslaved," reads 2 Peter 2:19 (RSV).

I'd never considered that I could be enslaved by my own thoughts. That is, not until God sent me a dog that forced me to live in the moment, and not in my brain.

That experience and everything that has followed in its wake has led me to a new understanding and appreciation for the wordless wisdom of God. Sometimes God's grace has to fly under our intellectual radar to get to our heart.

Or, as in my case, He can just use a dog.

"This is going to work out perfectly," I enthused to my husband as we packed our suitcases. "Gracie's at Doggy Boot Camp while we're in Europe. When we get back, we go twice to practice the training with her, and then we'll bring home our trained dog. I'll be able to walk with her anywhere, and we'll all live happily ever after."

"If that's all it takes to live happily ever after," he replied, "we're getting off easy."

I rolled up another shirt to stuff into my carry-on and checked the item off my packing list. Five days ago, I'd taken Gracie to Wings & Whistles and met our trainer, Mike. When I voiced my concern about the use of electronic collars for training, he readily demonstrated their use for me in order to relieve my fears.

"Here," he said, offering a collar for me to hold. "You can see for yourself what it feels like."

I looked at him in surprise as I took the collar. Was this standard procedure—offering to give clients a jolt? "You're going to shock me?" I asked.

He showed me where to place my fingers on the two prongs to complete the circuit. I wondered briefly if the shock would stop my heart, and if so, who was going to walk Gracie every day at lunch when Colleen returned to high school in the fall.

"Did you feel that?" he asked.

"Feel what?"

"The buzz," he replied. "Let's try it again."

He pressed the button on the remote control in his hand.

It was like a little zing across my fingertips.

"That's it?" I asked.

"We usually have to start out at a higher level, but once the dogs are responding, we drop it back. We want to use the least amount of stimulation."

I turned the collar over in my hand. It was simple, black, heavy-duty plastic, with a small boxlike housing on one side that contained the receiver and charge producer. No spikes, no wicked teeth. I mentally loaded a scale with the small jolt of electricity I'd felt versus the sheer pleasure I would find in walking an obedient Gracie every day for the rest of her life.

Gee, now that was a tough call.

"Let's do this," I said, shaking Mike's hand and giving Gracie a goodbye pat on the head.

"We'll be back in two weeks," I told them both, as Mike slipped a training lead over Gracie's head.

"You're going to Europe, right?"

I nodded. "England and Ireland. Tom will be working for the week at the company plant in Londonderry in Northern Ireland, while Colleen and I spend a few days in London. Then we'll fly to Belfast and take a car to meet Tom in Londonderry. It will be quite the adventure for us, I'm sure."

As I finished packing my suitcase, I marveled at how far we would travel in the next twenty-four hours. I'd start the day in Minnesota and eat breakfast in London. Not being much of a traveler, let alone an international one, the trip before me loomed large and exciting.

Yet I'd already come much further in the last four months than I ever would have expected, thanks to Gracie's influence. Tom had wanted me to accompany him to Ireland for years, but I'd always found excuses not to go. "It's the school year, I can't leave Colleen with someone else," or "we could use the money in much better ways than to pay for a trip for me I don't need," or "I traveled when I was a kid, so I don't need to go now."

The truth, though, was that I was afraid—afraid to move beyond the comfort zone and predictability of my ordered, safe life. I didn't trust myself to step into the unknown . . . because I didn't, ultimately, trust that God would be with me.

Oh, I knew intellectually that God was faithful. I'd spent four years getting my master's degree in theological studies under the tutelage of expert professors who were also devoted Christians. I'd read and studied the Bible. I'd learned to parse out the meaning of Scripture and set it into historical and critical context. As an active member of my church community, I'd taught faith formation classes for years and led adult faith renewal sessions. It was in the course of one of those sessions that I began to feel inadequate to the task of investigating and sharing my faith; so much so, that I decided I wanted to go back to college at the age of 44 and commit myself to a serious study of Christianity and what it meant for me.

Looking back, I guess I thought that if I studied and learned enough academic material about God, I'd pick the winning number in the spiritual lottery and wake up one morning filled with the Holy Spirit.

It didn't happen. What was it going to take to feel truly united with God? Why couldn't I just *think* myself closer to God?

I ruminated about that, too, which, of course, made my lack of faith even more upsetting!

The day I plunged into the ravine to retrieve our errant dog changed my life. I dropped my ruminations and anxiety and trust issues on the edge of the woods and focused completely, solely, on the moment. Every time I ventured out with Gracie since then was, in reality, more practice for me—practice in shutting out all the human-induced noise in my head so I could pay close attention to what a big black dog needed. Along the way, I learned that the quieter my mind got, the more focused I became on looking outward instead of inward, and the more I could hear and see God's presence around me.

It was the opposite of what I'd done for so long. Instead of filling my head, I needed to empty it out.

"How can you be afraid of death?" my husband had asked me as I began to panic in the surgery prep suite before my angiogram. "You know God loves you. You know Jesus. You believe in heaven."

"I do," I'd cried. "I'm just afraid of how I get there."

But his challenging words stayed with me, and after I went home, my heart unquestionably sound, I acknowledged to myself that my faith was not what I had hoped it was.

And I didn't know the way to make it better.

It took me months with a dog to realize that it wasn't about "knowing" at all.

It was about "being."

Being open to every moment, every person, every opportunity, and experiencing everything as new and fresh and blessed. It was about wagging my tail and saying "Yes!" every time a door opened, whether it was literal or figurative. It was about putting my brain back in balance with my other senses and nature itself in order to be whole and wholly Christ's, which is where God wants me—and, I believe, everyone—to be.

"God saw all that he had made—and it was very good!" reads Genesis 1:31. Just how good His creation was is becoming increasingly evident as medical researchers dig deeply into the healing effect of the natural world on human illness and disease.

Look at plants, for example.

Aside from traditional pharmacological uses of plant-based substances to treat everything from the common cold to post-thrombotic syndrome, plants have long been appreciated for their natural healing effects and their role in creating healthy environments. Plants such as aloe vera, golden pothos, and chrysanthemums, among many others, filter indoor air of harmful formaldehyde and benzene, found in many chemical cleaning products. The effectiveness of horticultural therapy was first documented in the nineteenth century as a treatment for mentally ill patients; today, it's also widely utilized in cognitive, vocational, and physical rehabilitation programs. Gardening, with its emphasis on growing and nurturing and hands-on participation, is good for the body as well as the soul.

Animal-assisted therapy (AAT) is likewise proving to be a successful—and natural—healing strategy in settings that range from hospitals and schools to nursing facilities and private homes. Unlike "service" animals that are trained to assist disabled owners with specific life activities, therapy animals are used to support a person's physical and emotional healing. Goats, sheep, horses, pigs, cats, dogs, dolphins, parrots, chickens, and hamsters are all popular animal "therapists", and even camels and at least one watusi (an African breed of cattle) have joined the ranks of nonhuman practitioners.[9]

(I've even read articles about massage therapists who use snakes to deliver deep tissue massage. I know that my son's cat gives a great localized kneading when it curls up on my lap, but a snake? I don't think so. Tell you what—if you decide to give it a try, let me know how it turns out . . .).

Dogs in particular, however, have most often been noted for their therapeutic effects on humans. Multiple medical studies have documented reduced stress and physical pain levels in patients after time spent with therapy dogs, while similar research at nursing homes found a marked decrease in residents' negative behaviors such as withdrawal and loneliness, and Increased verbal communication and social participation during animal visits. At the other end of the age spectrum, the company of a dog has been shown to improve children's literacy skills. For example, in her book *Every Dog Has a Gift: True Stories of Dogs Who Bring Hope & Healing Into Our Lives*, Rachel McPherson, founder and executive director of the Good Dog Foundation, includes two stories about dogs and young readers. At Gabriel's Angels in Arizona, the healing presence of dogs is put to the service of 13,000 at-risk children in testimony to the agency's conviction that the "unconditional love of a dog can heal a child."[10]

To my mind, what is perhaps most stunning about all of these animal-assisted therapies is that they employ God's creatures to heal fellow creatures. Animals can help restore wounded humans, whether they are combat veterans suffering from the aftermath of war, children who lack self-confidence, or seniors who feel disconnected from life. By drawing on the resources God has provided in creation, people can find balance and wholeness, hope and healing. Humans and animals, along with the other gifts of the earth, are not competitors in some kind of reality show contest, but complementary creations designed to work together to bring about God's kingdom.

If that's not proof of intelligent design by the Creator, I don't know what is.

I recently had the pleasure of meeting Meg Daley Olmert, author of *Made for Each Other: The Biology of the Animal-Human Bond* at a conference at the Minnesota Landscape Arboretum near my home. As one of the featured speakers, Olmert reviewed the research on oxytocin's chemical effects on humans, and the role those effects have played in human-animal bonding. Based on the powerful hormonal, physical, and psychological benefits that oxytocin induces in both a mother and her nursing infant, Olmert believes that this neurobiological dynamic is a "clear, quantifiable example of how to give is to receive." Later, when I asked her to expand on that idea, she shared her conviction that, "All together, I feel this creates a picture that, biologically, it is more blessed to give than to receive. And leads me to suggest that oxytocin is the biological equivalent or manifestation of 'Grace.'"

Which leads me to ask: Did God design our dogs to bring us closer to Him?

Judging from my healing experience with my own dog, I think so. And while it's intriguing to learn that science affirms how good God made our dogs, I don't know if any happy dog owner ever doubted it.

Although I do have to wonder just how thick God knows my skull to be. He did, after all, send me a dog *named* Grace.

Well, duh.

Chapter 8

Testing: one, two, three

We sit down to dinner. Tom and I sit on one side of the table, and Colleen is seated across from us. Gracie sits on her haunches on the rug, positioning herself equally between Tom's and Colleen's chairs. She silently watches every bite they take with rapt attention.

"Thanks for dinner, Mom," Colleen says when everyone is finished eating.

Gracie scoots closer to Colleen's side of the table.

"It was really good," Colleen adds, her eyes keeping contact with mine as she smoothly hands a scrap of steak to Gracie under the table.

"I saw that," I tell her.

Colleen smiles apologetically. "I know."

She cuts up the last bits on her plate and offers them to the dog, one at a time. Gracie gladly accepts each one.

After finishing her last bite, Gracie shifts to the other side of the table and looks at Tom imploringly.

"You know I have something for you, don't you?" He hands her part of a freshly baked buttermilk biscuit, which she happily downs in one swallow. She gazes adoringly into my husband's eyes.

Gracie, we found out early on, loves buttermilk biscuits.

"Whatever happened to our rule of not feeding her from the table?" I ask.

"What rule was that?" he replies, feigning innocence. He hands her the last of the biscuit.

When we stand up to clear the table of the dishes, Gracie barks once.

"She wants her Kong," I say. I go to the kitchen drawer where we keep her Kong toy and the beef sticks. I break up two sticks and stuff them into the center cavity of the hard rubber Kong, then go and lay the toy on the rug in front of the dog. Gracie waits for me to straighten up and give her permission to take the toy.

"You can have it," I tell her, nodding at the Kong. She picks it up in her teeth and shakes it to loosen the sticks inside. A few pieces fall out, and she drops the Kong to grab the beef. It takes her another forty seconds to get the remaining pieces out. I finish putting whatever leftovers we have—usually just a few vegetables since everything else, Gracie will eat—in the refrigerator just in time to see her stand by the table and give me a meaningful look.

I stare back and she barks.

"I know," I tell her. "It's time for a walk." I grab the leash and we go outside.

Tom and Colleen aren't the only ones Gracie has trained well.

As it turns out, effectively training a dog is a two-way street. You teach the dog desired behaviors by constantly monitoring its responses to your directions and correcting when necessary.

I got the term "correcting" from our trainer Mike at Wings & Whistles. I like the concept of "correcting" a lot. It makes me feel good about my desire to help Gracie adjust her behavior to make us all happy housemates. It reminds me of the positive reinforcement strategies we used on our children. Instead of looking at training as a harsh process that involves reward and punishment, "correcting" sounds all touchy-feely.

Of course, in the beginning of her training, Mike was using an electronic collar that delivered a mild shock to Gracie every time she didn't comply with his commands, and I have no doubt that Gracie would not have termed it "touchy-feely." For all I know, she was cursing a doggy blue streak every time Mike touched the button. But the fact is, she came home to us trained, and that made everyone happy. Go ahead and accuse me of turning a blind eye to a barbaric method of imposing human will on a helpless animal, but in this situation, the end totally justified the means. The end being that Gracie will never have to see the inside of another animal shelter for as long as she lives, because I can now—thanks to her training—manage her behavior on a daily basis and guarantee her physical safety.

It's the day we bring Gracie home from her stint at Doggy Boot Camp. Since returning from vacation, we've come out to Wings & Whistles to participate in two short training sessions with Gracie and her trainer. Mike has taught us the proper way to walk the dog, along with when and how to use the collar for continued training purposes. Over time, with practice and consistency on our part, Gracie's responses to our commands will become so ingrained that we won't need to use the collar to insure her obedience. In the immediate weeks to come, however, we might need to remind her that we demand the same responses that she gives Mike. That means she needs to walk (or run) at our pace at our heels, come when called (the first time, not the fifth or sixth), and always keep within our sight. If she balks, we'll give her a small buzz with her collar to keep her on the straight and narrow.

Colleen and I wait outside the kennel building for Mike to bring Gracie out to us. The door opens, and out they come, Gracie pacing herself right at his heel. She sees us and runs over to greet us with a wagging tail and several play bows. Yesterday when we arrived, Gracie literally jumped for joy to see us again and practically knocked us flat on our backs. Today, though, she's already learned to temper her exuberance with good manners.

"She's a smart dog," Mike comments.

I figure he tells all the dog owners that, but I don't interrupt. I can't imagine a dog trainer telling a client that her dog is stupid, even if said dog was as dumb as it looks. Bad for repeat business, you know.

"And she's high energy."

I nod. I'd figured that one out pretty quickly myself. I'm not as dumb as I look, either.

"She's a real tomboy," Mike adds. He explains that some female dogs are prissy or refuse to play rough, but not our Gracie. She loves to mix it up with the tough boys.

I nod again. At the dog park, her favorite playmates are the big dogs, and the more they want to grapple and wrestle, the happier she is. And if they're willing to roll around in the mud with her, even better.

"Yes," I agree, "I don't think we'll be getting her pink tutus and tiaras to wear anytime soon."

"Remember what I told you about being consistently firm with her," he repeats one last time. "She'll test you every chance she gets."

I nod again and shake his hand in farewell. "Thank you so much, Mike. This has made all the difference in the world for us."

I turn to Gracie. "Heel," I tell her as we walk to the car.

She trots right beside me, her ears and nose up.

I don't even have the leash on her.

She's that good.

I reach for the car door handle and she patiently waits for me to open it. "Get in," I tell her, and she promptly complies. She immediately sits on her haunches in the back seat on the driver's side, her eyes forward.

I wonder if she'll buckle herself in if I tell her to.

"This is amazing," I say to Colleen who is already seated in the passenger seat. "Did you see that? She didn't throw herself in the car like she used to do, not to mention heeling without a leash. It's like a miracle."

"It's going to be a lot easier to walk her now," Colleen agrees.

"It's a whole new world," I enthuse. "We have a trained dog!"

Remember a while back when I said that effectively training a dog is a two-way street?

Actually, it's more like a busy intersection.

Yes, you tell the dog what to do, the dog responds, and you feel like the best dog owner ever. You're more than satisfied with the money you spent on having your dog trained.

At the same time, however, you're doing exactly what the dog has trained *you* to do in response to its response. You teach the dog desired behaviors by constantly monitoring its responses to your directions and correcting when necessary. Over time, the dog also learns what your reaction will be to its response. It's like when you raise your kids.

You go to the grocery store, a toddler in tow. He gets tired and whiny. You think about leaving immediately, but then you won't get your shopping done, so you try to cajole the child with soothing words.

Like that ever helps.

Junior knows the drill. He will continue to whine, and you will get more frantic to calm him down, until you cave and buy him the juice box, or cookie, or kitchen tool he loves.

(No joke, I saw a mom hand a kid who was in full melt-down mode a kitchen strainer, and he was totally satisfied and quiet for the rest of the trip down the aisle. I wish my kids had cried for kitchen tools—I was always short of slotted spoons and spatulas.)

You get what you want. Junior gets what he wants. Everybody's happy, and you play this scene out for years.

Make that decades.

Thank goodness Gracie will never need a car.

The point is that your child learns how to push your buttons in the proper sequence to get a certain result. You let it happen because in the terrifying and vast landscape of parenting, you've learned to pick your battles, and this one just isn't worth the struggle. Trust me, buying the cookie is nothing compared to enforcing a teen's curfew.

Dogs do the same thing. (Although the good news here is that curfew is never an issue with the dog.) Like the grocery store routine we used to do with the kids, the dinner scene I described at the beginning of this chapter is a finely tuned choreography we perform every night. After countless rehearsals, we've learned to eliminate the whining (on the parts of both the dog and the human participants) and move smoothly through the dinner hour. Gracie knows she will get scraps if she waits politely and quietly as a reward for her behavior. Tom, Colleen, and I know that we can eat in peace because of it, and so we are happy to supply her with those same scraps from the table. In the process, we have learned something important and humbling about ourselves: we can all be trained by a dog.

After Gracie came home from Doggy Boot Camp, I followed our trainer's instructions religiously. Mike had impressed upon us the importance of continuing to work with her every day, even if all we did was spend fifteen minutes heeling in circles. Before every walk, I buckled on her electronic collar and looped the remote control over my head, though I rarely used it since her behavior was exemplary. On the few occasions Gracie didn't immediately comply with my commands, I gave her a short buzz at the collar's lowest level, and she hopped to it. Unlike our previous walking experiences, Gracie easily made complete trips all the way home, and instead of feeling like I'd been dragged around the block only to be stranded a couple doors away with a stubborn dog that wouldn't move, I came to thoroughly enjoy our strolls in the neighborhood.

In fact, now that I knew how a well-trained dog should behave on a walk, I couldn't help but notice when I saw other dogs pulling their masters and mistresses around the block, straining hard on the leash and then making abrupt stops.

"That dog needs some training," I'd observe, proud of Gracie's perfect position at my heel. "They should go see Mike."

I was so proud of our dog, and so deliriously happy with her transformation into a good walker that I did the worst possible thing the very first time she didn't come at my first call.

I let it slide.

I didn't correct her.

I just called her again, at which point, she came.

"No problem," I told myself. "It's not like she's a show dog. She doesn't have to come every time, the first time. She's obedient enough."

Seriously, Gracie wasn't the one who needed the collar to remind her of her training. Mike should have given *me* one.

Despite my poor dog-training maintenance skills, Gracie is obedient enough for us. She walks well on a leash, mainly because I'm never in a rush when I walk her. She's a dog, with a big nose, and since I know that through her nose is how she best experiences her world, I'm content to let her sniff her way around the neighborhood when we go for a walk. If she wants to pick up the pace and trot, I'll keep up with her—I tell myself she's earning her keep as my physical trainer. If I feel like running, she'll run with me. Maybe she thinks I'm "obedient enough," too.

Gracie does not, however, always come on the first call.

Or the second.

By the third time, the odds definitely improve.

Yet if I call to her with urgency in my voice, Gracie responds immediately. Like every dog, she has learned the nuances of her master's tone, and she knows to whom she belongs. We may not be the winners of the Best in Show ribbon in the centuries-long history of dog and owner, but we've certainly schooled ourselves to be attuned to each other.

And that makes both of us happy.

Now, *that's* harmony.

It's also good communication.

Every skilled communicator will tell you that speaking is only half the job, with listening being the other half. While that works pretty well for most humans (note that I qualified that with "most"—I'm still unsure where mono-syllabic teenaged boys fit in any kind of communications model), dogs are a breed apart.

Make that a "species" apart.

As a result, human communication strategies don't always apply to dogs. Let me give you an example.

For many years, my husband and I helped prepare couples for marriage in our church. Part of the preparation was an exercise in reflective listening as an approach to conflict resolution.

We'd choose one area in which the couple wanted to improve, and we'd walk them through using "I" statements to clarify the underlying feelings that were causing the conflict.

"Okay," I'd say to the bride-to-be. "On the couple's survey you took, you said your fiancé doesn't listen to you. I want you to make an 'I' statement about that to him."

Bride-to-be takes a deep breath and looks at fiancé. "You don't listen to me."

"I don't," the fiancé quickly affirms. He tells my husband, "I don't care what she thinks."

"You need to tell *her*," my husband directs, nodding toward the bride-to-be.

The young man faces his intended. "I don't care what you think."

A stunned silence fills the room.

"Okay, then," my husband says. "I think that clarifies the conflict, don't you?"

"She didn't use an 'I' statement," the fiancé points out. "No wonder we have trouble communicating."

On second thought, that's probably not a good example.

But it does illustrate one key human communication technique that dogs can't use—they can't make "I" statements or bring reflective listening into a conversation. Since dogs don't have the vocal chords, lips, or palates we have, their verbal language is limited to a repertoire of barks, growls or whines—all of which may hold clear meaning for other dogs, without a single articulated "I" in there anywhere. The ability to produce specific noises and pitches in response to stimuli may all qualify as generic dog-speak to us, but in reality, they are canine comments in specific situational contexts.[11]

In addition, dogs can, and do, use body language, an example of which, incidentally, our bride-to-be clearly demonstrated when she subsequently stomped out of our session. Dogs, in fact, employ a very sophisticated system of body language that humans are only now beginning to document. Along with their vocalizations, the positioning of dogs' bodies and tails constitutes a canine language that can not only be witnessed by discerning and patient humans, but in many instances, appreciated and understood.

One of the books I read in the week immediately following Gracie's adoption gave me much-needed insight into the world of canine non-verbal communication. Acting on a tip I received from another dog owner I met at the dog park soon after, I got a copy of *Inside of a Dog* by cognitive psychologist Alexandra Horowitz. Aside from teaching me that Gracie learned about the world primarily through her nose, the book inspired me to closely watch her physical responses to all types of sensory stimuli, from the familiar sound of the tread of my husband's feet on the stairs to the whiff of another dog walking by the house to a glimpse of my car keys.

After two years, my constant study of her posture and behavior has now yielded me a keen awareness of Gracie's needs and wants. I know the subtleties in her bark and whine. I know when she's not feeling well and when she scents a coyote somewhere near the neighborhood during our evening walk. I think I can even tell when she begins to recognize that we're headed for her favorite day-care facility in the car; whether she associates the intonation in my voice when I tell her the destination, or she smells the particular vegetation that lines the route there, I'm convinced she knows where we're going.

I think I've learned to "listen" to our dog, and not rely so much on talking.

Gee, maybe future dog owners should be required to take some kind of preparation class in dog communication. We could start with reflective barking.

Woof.

Learning to communicate with Gracie has demanded as much focus on my part as it did when I was taking instruction from Mike at Wings & Whistles on how to manage and correct Gracie's behavior. In both cases, I've learned that training is only as good as the discipline you commit to it every day and that you truly reap what you sow. Honestly, it doesn't bother me that Gracie doesn't always walk precisely at my heel now, but I know she could do better.

She did do better, until I relaxed my standards of obedience. It wasn't the training regimen that failed. It was the human.

Sometimes, I wonder if I cut her some slack in discipline because I know I'm not perfect, either.

Not that I don't want to do better, especially as a Christian.

Actually, I want very much to do better. I know the key lies in my commitment to discipline, just as success with training Gracie depends on my consistency. The same scriptural instruction comes back to mind: "Train up a child in the way he should go, and when he is old he will not depart from it" (Proverbs 22:6, NKJV).

He may, however, take some detours—I know I have. The challenge, I'm finding, is recommitting to training, to Christian discipline, in every stage of my life.

Every day.

Like Gracie, I still need correction, but in my case, my Trainer has a capital "T". I'm a work-in-progress as much as any dog in training, and when I keep my focus on my Master, obedience sets me free.

Thankfully, though, I don't need dog treats for my reward.

Chapter 9

Where does the fried chicken come from, anyway?

Speaking of food, my dog believes there is a fried chicken fairy.

I'm beginning to believe it now, too. This morning, for the second time in two months, Gracie found pieces of fried chicken during our morning walk through the neighborhood. Gracie loves fried chicken, and if she could, I think she'd hotwire every vehicle in sight in order to drive to the closest deli for fried chicken.

"Give me a box of fried chicken," she'd say (though it would sound more like *rrrruff*!) as she plastered herself against the deli case.

"For here or to go?" the overworked deli clerk would ask, thinking to herself that she really needed to find a different job when the customers started looking like dogs.

As it is, I buy the deli chicken for dinner about every six weeks, and I give Gracie the meat from the drumsticks and wings, even though she'd much rather eat the whole thing, bones included.

So finding complete chicken pieces on our morning walk must be like winning the lottery to her. She grabs those pieces and starts crunching before I even realize it's in her mouth. Because I need my fingers for typing and other manual tasks, I don't try to pull the chicken out of her mouth. But it makes me crazy that she's eating it, because I'm afraid it's spoiled and will make her sick. True, it's colder outside than the inside of my refrigerator's freezer compartment (literally), but still, I don't want her eating anything when I don't know where it came from, or whose mouth it already encountered.

Speaking of which, how in the world the fried chicken ends up along the sidewalk is beyond me. I just can't see any of my neighbors tossing chicken pieces out in their yards, especially when it's been below freezing for the last few months. We may be Minnesotans, but I don't know anyone who's picnicking at three degrees Fahrenheit. Do people drive into our neighborhood to throw out the fried chicken they can't finish? Is that anything like leaving odd pieces of furniture on a street corner in the dead of night with a 'FREE' sign on it?

Or is there really a fried chicken fairy that Gracie has conjured through her own wishful thinking?

Hmmm.

I wish, wish, wish there was a *piña colada* fairy . . .

I have learned two important things about provenance since Gracie has come into my life:

1. *No matter how hard you try, wishing doesn't make anything so. Cases in point: The most desperate wishing I've ever wished couldn't make Gracie get off her rear end and walk home. Also, I have yet to find any evidence of a piña colada fairy in or around my neighborhood.*

2. *Allowing God to supply my needs on His own terms can be faith-trying, but ultimately incredibly rewarding and soul-expanding. Gracie is both sign and proof of this to me. I never would have chosen a dog, of all things, to help me find God again, but that was clearly the plan. Not only did it work, but God's creative choice grew my personal horizons far beyond what they'd been before my crisis of faith. It has also made me very happy.*

And now I think this is the part of the book I've been avoiding—the part where the pride comes in.

As in human pride, not like a pride of lions.

Although it would be much easier to talk about lions: majestic creatures roaming the savannah, roaring in the night, chasing down prey in nature's own unending drama of life and death. We could make it a mini-series. Or a movie.

Wait, Disney studios already did that.

Talking about human pride, and especially *my* human pride, though, is awkward and embarrassing. No night-vision photography or catchy tunes involved. I have to cut right to the bone and expose in myself an insidious weakness that no one likes to admit.

Pride.

As I look back at how I reacted to my heart scare, I realize now that I never completely trusted God to take care of me because I was too proud to admit I couldn't meet all my own needs.

That I wasn't in complete control of my life.

That I was . . . mortal.

What a surprise.

There's a reason that pride is known as the original sin, and was such a big hit on the ancient Greek stages. No one can escape pride; we all suffer from it. We suffer *with* it. It's a condition of our humanness. As soon as an individual becomes aware of his or her individual-ness, the "me" word becomes a driving force of organization for every effort. In other words, we think we're pretty hot stuff, and we give ourselves the credit for it, instead of giving it to God.

And that's what I'd forgotten until a stress test said my heart was flawed.

The rest was wrong, but in essence, the diagnosis was right.

My heart *was* flawed, because it was focused on me, not on God. I was an adult. I was responsible. I'd raised five kids and been a faithful woman. I'd even studied theology so I'd know God better.

I, I, I.

Does any of this sound even remotely familiar to you?

It reminds me of one of my husband's favorite sayings: "All your problems have one thing in common: you."

I just don't think I was aware I had a problem, until Gracie came into my life to fix it.

I looked at the clock on the bookcase and groaned.

"Really, Gracie? Nine at night?"

Gracie fixed her sternest stare on me, lowered her head and barked once. I was sure I could see her slight tip of the head toward the front door of the living room.

I glanced at Tom and Colleen, both of whom were already dressed for bed and deep into books. I sighed and pulled my jacket out of the closet.

"Why am I the one going out into the dark when I'm not the one who asked for the dog?" I muttered to myself. I snapped the leash onto Gracie's collar and out we went into the brisk night air.

For the first block of our walk, I mentally rehearsed all the angry things I wanted to say to my husband and daughter. Things like "How come I don't get to change into pajamas and lounge around for the rest of the night?" and "I'd like a night off too, sometime." Yes, I knew that Colleen wasn't comfortable walking outside alone at night (even though she'd have a big dog with her). And by the end of the day, Tom's pronated ankles made it painful for him to walk, which was why, by Gracie's first autumn with us, I'd become the default evening walker. Yet I still struggled with it, and despite my sound rationalizations for it, I was angry with the situation.

I'd been tagged with a job I didn't want, and hadn't asked for.

But as happened to me every night, by the time we turned back toward home, I'd calmed down about the injustice of getting saddled with Gracie's evening walk, and instead, found myself star-gazing and thanking God for the beauty of the night sky I would otherwise have missed. Without Gracie demanding a final stroll, I knew I would never have stepped outside in the cold just to admire the night and take a few deep breaths.

God, though, knew I needed it, and ever faithful, He supplied it.

"For as high as the heavens are above the earth, so great is his love for those who fear him," I reminded myself (Psalm 103:11). How simple it was to let God take care of me and all my needs! Buoyed by God's generosity, I resolved not to complain about night walking. So it surprised me when I walked back into the house . . . and immediately confronted Tom and Colleen with my angry feelings.

"I need to say something to you both," I said, even as I marveled at my unexpected nerve.

For the briefest moment in time, I wondered if I was having an out-of-body experience, since this was certainly way out of character for me. I'd always been the nice mom, the agreeable volunteer, the easy-going employee.

I worked at being invisible.

But I'd thought it was the Christian way to be, always being kind and turning the other cheek. On top of that, I'd grown up with the take-charge attitude that if something was going to be done right, you had to do it yourself.

God helps those who help themselves, right? (Or so said Ben Franklin, who popularized the ancient—but extra-biblical—phrase.)

Yet here I was, about to tell my husband and daughter that I couldn't do it all anymore.

I was fallible.

I needed help.

I couldn't do it alone.

The realization that I was finally going to admit it and ask for help almost closed my throat.

I pushed the words out. "I feel like I'm the only one taking responsibility for Gracie," I told Tom and Colleen. "I don't think it's fair, and I want it to change. I can't do it anymore by myself. That's all I have to say."

Funny thing was, it *was* all I had to say. Tom and Colleen agreed to take turns doing the evening walk. Colleen started carrying a flashlight until she was comfortable outside at night with Gracie. Tom paced himself during the day to alleviate some of his foot pain so he could take short walks with Gracie in the evening.

I got to put on my pajamas before eight o'clock.

And now, sometimes, I switch turns with Tom or Colleen, just so I can go outside in the dark, my dog beside me, and marvel at the starry skies and the amazing provenance of God.

A few weeks ago, I mentioned to Tom that I liked to stay up late and work alone in our basement.

"I get so much done with no distractions," I explained. "And I feel safe because Gracie hangs out with me. I don't worry about someone breaking in, because they'd have to deal with a big black barking dog."

Tom laughed. "Who would have thought that the dog that once terrified you, now makes you feel safe?"

Actually, since I've started learning about human-animal bonding, I can think of several people, beginning with American biologist and two-time Pulitzer Prize winner E. O. Wilson.

A former Harvard professor, Wilson is perhaps best known for his groundbreaking work in the study of the biological causes of social behavior, which he termed "sociobiology." Based on his research, he suggests that humans are genetically wired to be attracted to, and to bond with, other living things, which he describes in his 1984 book *Biophilia*.[12] While he does not make any religious claims with his biophilia hypothesis, a Christian interpretation can be easily constructed, especially in light of current developments in Christian thought regarding ecotheology and stewardship, which calls all of us to responsible interaction with all of creation as an obligation of our faith.

To state it most simply, humanity is part of God's creation, but in order to realize the fullness of the life He created and models in Jesus Christ, humanity needs to meaningfully connect with all the works of God. The great English poet John Donne was correct in saying that "no man is an island entire of itself"; in many ways, today's ecological and conservation movements have taken up this same cry as they challenge people to champion and preserve the natural world. Wilson, in his theories, seems to suggest that the plan for preservation, the path to restoration, is no mystery, because we have already been designed to seek life, if only we would open our hearts and minds to what already exists within us: the blueprint for seeking, and making, the connections that he believes are etched into our DNA.

Life calls to life.

Connecting with life itself, heeding our DNA, is why people find healing in nature, whether it's in the form of planting a tree or cleaning up waterways, stroking a chicken or hugging a dog. God wants each of us to be well and whole, and He's provided the means for us to do so, not the least of which are plants to heal us and animals for us to love. Why not use the gifts that God has given us? Why else would the oxytocin exchange exist between animals, if not as a divine system for allowing fellow creatures to cultivate a friendship that benefits both?

Why sink your hands into the earth to plant flowers?

Because instinctually, spiritually, and biologically, we are designed to seek life.

We are the people of the God of Life.

"I am come that they might have life, and that they might have it more abundantly," says the Lord in John 10:10. During his entire ministry, Jesus modeled how to receive that life by finding God in all of creation and loving it. Jesus sought quality time with God amidst the setting of His creation of nature. Desert, mountaintop, olive grove or inland sea—Jesus found communion with God in all those places and was strengthened by it.

For our part, how often do we get away to connect with God in a peaceful natural setting?

And I'm not talking about sitting on your backyard porch as you say a quick prayer in between making phone calls or checking your email on your laptop.

How often do you invest in dedicated time with God's creation?

Even when I walk Gracie, more than half of the dog-walkers or runners I see are plugged into headsets or iPods, getting their exercise, but seemingly oblivious to the natural sounds and scenery around them. I feel sorry for them because they miss so much—the sound of geese calling for mates, the sight of their dog's nose quivering with the excitement of fleeting scents we can't begin to detect.

Yes, physical training is good for the body, but what about the spiritual side of wholeness? Too often, the outdoors is the background to our to-do list, rather than being celebrated as the main event itself. Is it any wonder that so many of us today, caught up in, and consumed by, our technological worlds of business, suffer from a host of illnesses, not least of which are depression and anxiety?

In his 2005 book, *Last Child in the Woods: Saving Our Children from Nature-Deficit Disorder*, child advocacy expert Richard Louv convincingly tracked down a contributing cause of a host of increasingly common childhood disorders, including depression, Attention Deficit Disorder, and obesity. Citing the reports of multiple studies, he contended that children have become disconnected from nature, and it is that broken relationship that accounts for many of the physical, emotional, and spiritual deficiencies that plague the younger generation.[13] Six years later, he extended that discussion to include the adult experience of nature deficit disorder in his book *The Nature Principle*, calling on people everywhere to return to the "restorative powers" of nature to help reshape the human condition.[14]

Seriously, if you could lower your stress level and add years to your life just by taking a quick walk through a greenbelt every day, wouldn't you be the first one out the door?

Add a dog at your heel, and your experience of quality of life would improve even more. That's not just dog-lovers sharing anecdotal evidence, either. Science has jumped on the growing interest in natural therapies and set itself to the task of identifying quantifiable results of the human connection with nature.

In *Your Brain on Nature: The Science of Nature's Influence on Your Health, Happiness, and Vitality*, Eva Selhub, MD, and Alan Logan, ND, have documented the positive effects of natural environments on the brain.[15] Combined with the findings of Louv, Olmert, and other researchers about the transformation that nature can effect on human behavior and neurophysiology, there can be no question that nature—God's creation—is good for humans.

The theologian in me wants to jump up and down, point at the science and say: "See! Here is the indisputable proof of our faith that there is a loving God who intimately cares for each one of us. How else can you explain that watching a beautiful sunset actually lights up the neuro pathways in our brain?"

Yes, nature heals! It heals because God has willed it to be so, has purposely and lovingly designed it to be the perfect remedy for humankind's own self-inflicted damage. What Louv calls a disconnection from nature, I term an alienation from our authentic place in God's creation. And while I'm not totally convinced that Isaiah 11:6 had it exactly right about the possible extent of all interspecies friendships—"the wolf also shall dwell with the lamb, and the leopard will lie down with a kid and a little child shall lead them" (RSV)—I am sure that humanity has a key role to play in bringing about lasting peace to the earth. I think it's about balancing human needs and wants with the integrity of the natural world, and if we could only learn to listen to God, we would know how to achieve it.

For me, the beginning of the path to restoring and reaping the benefits of that person-creation balance has been as simple as caring for a dog. Whether it's walking or grooming or feeding, the basic tasks of dog ownership bring me closer to God, and take me further away from my human-induced anxieties.

Thanks to Gracie, I've learned to walk around the neighborhood and notice the buds on the bushes and the pattern of tree bark while she buries her nose in a clump of grass to inhale the world as she knows it.

Because she has a big nose and loves to use it, believe me, I get a lot of time to observe those bushes and trees. In fact, I get to check in on them almost every day, all year round. I haven't yet named each one, though I won't be surprised when that happens judging from how familiar I'm becoming with them. So far, I've only given names to two things along our walking routes, and that is only because Gracie insisted on visiting them every time we passed by: Rocky's Remains and Ickey Mouse.

Moving right along . . .

Let me put it this way: by opening my senses to the smells, sights, sounds, and touch of the natural worlds that coexist with my human one, I experience a respect and awe of life itself that I've too often overlooked or ignored. Walks with Gracie, I've found, are blessed opportunities for prayers of praise and thanksgiving as I take the time to be overwhelmed by God's love, right here and right now.

Rain, snow, or sunshine—it's all good when I walk in it with Gracie.

Even if there is no fried chicken—or *piña colada*—fairy.

Chapter 10

Life! with a dog

Can I talk to you about a personal matter?

TICKS.

(Cue screams)

I hate ticks. Everyone does.

(More screams)

Except for maybe tickologists. That's the scientific name for people who study ticks. (Screams) Tickologists might like ticks. Or not. Do you have to like something to study it? I don't know.

Oh, and Brad Paisley might like ticks. He wrote a song about them. Well, actually, he wrote a song about using a come-on line about ticks. Not that he'd need a come-on line. He's gorgeous. And he married Kimberly Williams, who is also gorgeous. But I digress.

Ticks are the summertime bane of dog owners. (Screams) As a dog owner, I know this. In fact, I know it too well, since last week, a friend and I walked our dogs along the Minnesota River, and when I got home, I found exactly a gazillion ticks on my shoes, my legs and even on our couch. (Cue lots of screams)

Obviously, the ticks on the couch were courtesy of Gracie, since I did not take the couch on the walk with us. Gracie, thankfully, sheds the nasty ticks because she's been dosed with Frontline, a tick repellant. That does not stop her from bringing in the bloodthirsty little suckers, however. They get a free ride on her to invade my home.

People cannot use Frontline. My friend gave me a recipe for a tick repellant that is basically a bottle of vinegar, but I haven't tried it yet. I don't want to smell like vinegar. Also, she gave it to me AFTER we walked along the river and collected our gazillion ticks. Ah, thanks.

In light of the present tick population explosion, however, I no longer want to walk with Gracie on anything this summer but paved surfaces, which means roads, parking lots and sidewalks. Actually, I am now of the opinion that really wide sidewalks are one of the world's engineering marvels. I hated them in the winter because they were covered in ice and I was afraid to walk on them and fall on my rear end.

(I did, indeed, take several rump bumps in the course of the winter, which I'm sure were highly amusing to the motorists passing by. Slow-motion pratfalls have always been big crowd pleasers in physical comedy, after all. In fact, if this authoring gig doesn't pan out, I might look into slapstick as my next career.)

In the summer, however, sidewalks are like a demilitarized zone between the maniacal hordes of ticks (screams, please) waiting on either side in the grass to hijack unsuspecting humans. This, I've decided, is really why sidewalks were invented—to protect people from tick death.

Thank you, sidewalk inventor.

Now if I could just come up with a way to dissuade the ticks from hitching a ride on Gracie, my couch would be tick-free.

Even if I'm not.

Finding ticks in our house is only one of the many new experiences that Gracie has brought into my life. Fortunately, most of the other new ones have been much more endearing than ticks.

Except for the rolling-in-fish aroma that one time. Even after two rinses, Gracie still stank up the whole house. Memo to me: for the rest of her life, do not let the dog roll in dead fish.

Other than that, life with Gracie continues to make me happy and healthier, and I can give you several obvious reasons for that: the successful operation of that mutual feedback loop of oxytocin that God ingeniously implanted in us, my physical health improvement thanks to ample exercise walking a dog, and the fact that I don't have the time or desire anymore to fixate on my own woes.

Having Gracie around, for me, is a lot like raising a houseful of kids, but without having to relearn how to solve algebraic equations every few years. I also don't have to referee sibling squabbles, or keep track of whose turn it is to choose what television show we watch. (Actually, I'm happy to report that Gracie and I have the same taste in television—the only show we watch is the annual Puppy Bowl. As far as I'm concerned, it's the only program on TV that's worth watching, and Gracie seems to agree since she can't take her eyes off the hamsters in the blimp.) I do have to wipe four muddy feet every time we come in from the rain, and sometimes Gracie doesn't want to come inside when it's time, but I don't have to listen to her complaining about it, either.

Because Gracie never complains. Gracie is a ray of sunshine that never quits.

And I want to be just like her.

Not the rolling in fish parts, of course. But the always-upbeat temperament part.

The total trust that life is good, that she is completely cared for, part.

Every morning when we get up, I still marvel at her unconditional delight in a new day as she bounds around the house, tail wagging, ears alert, and eyes bright. If I didn't know better,

I'd think she'd read the Bible and taken as her own credo the words in Matthew 6: 31-34: "So do not worry, saying 'What shall we eat?' or 'What shall we drink?' or 'What shall we wear?' For the pagans run after all these things, and your heavenly Father knows that you need them. But seek first his kingdom and his righteousness, and all these things will be given to you as well. Therefore do not worry about tomorrow, for tomorrow will worry about itself."

Frankly, I'm a little embarrassed that my dog demonstrates that kind of trust so much better than I do.

But I'm working on it. Gracie has set the bar for me, and I'm not ashamed to admit it.

Granted, I don't plan on shaking with excitement every time my husband grabs his car keys, but I'm getting much better about saying "yes" to new adventures, and throwing my obsessively excessive caution to the wind. When we traveled to Europe four months after adopting Gracie, for instance, I didn't bat an eye when my daughter and I got on the wrong bus in London and ended up riding through the locked-down section of town the morning after the 2011 riots that left burned-out buildings and shattered storefronts along the bus line. A year earlier, I wouldn't have considered a trip to London at all, let alone tried to navigate my way around an unfamiliar capital city the day after a night of sudden violence.

Heck, a year earlier, I was afraid to drive to downtown Minneapolis, and I only live twenty minutes away.

What a difference a dog made.

Before I had a dog, I heard all the stories about their devotion, their joyfulness, their never-ending optimism, their goofiness, their heart-tugging adorableness. As a dog-averse person, I chalked up those traits to the species' limited intelligence and the human inclination to "ooh" and "ahhh" over babies and helpless creatures.

I should probably clarify that last statement. When I referred to the "species' limited intelligence," I was talking about the dogs' intelligence, not the humans', although I have to admit, I often thought people were idiots to own dogs. I mean, why would you choose to scoop poop and live with a smelly dog that routinely ate your slippers and then vomited them back up on your carpet?

Now that I've learned about the scientific research, though, I know that the oohing behavior is the result of the hormone oxytocin flooding our systems, leading us to the compassionate responses that will nurture and insure the survival of our babies; cute helpless puppies are lucky enough to be able to push those same buttons in our biology and get the benefit of that same response.

That's the perspective of science.

My perspective is different, now that I live with a dog.

I think that dogs are gifts that teach us, if we let them, how to so totally trust God that we, too, would embrace every moment with a grin on our face and a happy wag in our tail.

Not only that, but I think that my relationship with Gracie is God's plan for me and for all human beings to share in *His* grace.

Not that I think Gracie is going to be everyone's dog. She can't be—she's as skilled at bilocation as I am, which is nil.

What I mean to say is that I think by building a positive relationship with God's gifts of creation, we regain harmony in our lives. Dogs and cats, backyard gardens and remote jungles—everything that God has made is part of our shared identity as creation. We are made in God's image, which is abundance incarnate; as His people, we are enmeshed in all of creation. And if we are at odds with any of creation, then we are, by definition, out of harmony with ourselves, causing us (and the rest of creation) distress, anxiety and the diminishment of God's grace. If we can begin to right that imbalance by adopting a pet, or planting a tree, we should rejoice at the opportunity and take it.

"He who is faithful in a very little thing is faithful also in much," Luke 16:10 reminds us, and God rewards our faithfulness (NET). In fact, His generosity is overflowing; I never would have dreamed of all the blessings that have poured into my life since I adopted a dog. I'm healthier—physically, mentally, and emotionally—and happier than I've ever been. The new friends and acquaintances I've met through my dog (are there any studies about dogs as social directors?) have become my treasured companions, enriching my life in ways I never imagined. God has opened new worlds to me, healed me, and drawn me closer to Himself, by working through a dog no one wanted.

Including me.

But now, I thank God every day for bringing me a dog, because now . . . well, now I live with Grace.

A final note . . .

---

*Y*ou know what I hope you do after reading my story about Gracie?

I hope you go out and adopt a rescued dog.

Not that I have anything against cats or horses or guinea pigs or anacondas, but they just don't interact with humans to the extent that a dog does. When it comes to a companion animal, dogs are the most companionable and portable. I've always loved cats, but I never had one that was jumping up and down with excitement to take a walk with me around the block on a leash. I like horses, too, but they don't fit in the house very well, and guinea pigs are . . . well . . . shaggy things in a cage.

As for anacondas, I admit I have absolutely no experience with them, and I hope it stays that way. I'm sure you can read all about them on the internet. Have at it.

I also have nothing against adopting a dog from a breeder. That way you get exactly the traits you're looking for, and you probably can predict fairly well what the dog will be like.

With a rescued dog, it's the luck of the draw. Since most of these dogs aren't purebreds, their personalities can be all over the map, but also because they aren't purebreds, you rarely have to worry about the health issues that can be inherent in certain pedigrees. Everyone I know who has adopted rescued dogs has been very happy with the outcome; whether the dogs are just so happy to finally be in a loving home with people who take good care of them, or they are just good-natured naturally, I can only guess. For all I know, maybe dogs that have been strays or abandoned or neglected simply have such low expectations based on prior experiences that anything represents an improvement and makes them deliriously grateful.

(True confession: this worked really well for us when our five kids were all little. You'd be amazed at how great a road trip with a car full of kids can be when it's only three hours long. Like I said, low expectations.)

What I like to think about rescued dogs is that God gives us a chance to do good when we take in a dog in need of a "forever home," as so many animal adoption agencies call it. And then, as in the case with every Christian act of love, we receive back, in measure overflowing, what we have given.

No, not dog biscuits.

Love.

Healing.

Trust.

Joy.

We become whole, and in so doing, we make the world a better place.

Yes, you might have to walk in the rain, you'll definitely need to scoop up poop, and occasionally, you'll pull a midnight shift caring for a sick dog, but life will be better than you ever believed it could be.

Trust me. I've been there, done that, and I'm still thanking God every day for my life . . . and for Grace.

Jan loves hearing from readers about
their own experiences with canine
companions, and she welcomes
opportunities as an event speaker to
encourage others to open their hearts
and homes to rescued pets.
Visit her on the web at
jandunlap.com
or email your comments to
mailbox@jandunlap.com.

Endnotes

Chapter 4

1. E Friedmann, A H Katcher, J J Lynch, and S A Thomas. "Animal companions and one-year survival of patients after discharge from a coronary care unit." *Public Health Reports*. 1980 Jul-Aug; 95(4): 307–312. Retrieved 2/28/2012 online from http://www.ncbi.nlm.nih.gov/pmc/articles/PMC1422527/?page=5

2. Baun MM, Bergstrom N, Langston NF, Thoma L. "Physiological effects of human/companion animal bonding."Nurse Res. 1984 May-Jun;33(3):126-9. Retrieved 2/28/2013 from http://www.ncbi.nlm.nih.gov/pubmed/6563527

3. Weizmann Institute of Science (2011, November 8). "New role for 'hormone of love' oxytocin in brain: Helps direct development of brain-body interface." *Science Daily*. Retrieved March 5, 2013, from http://www.sciencedaily.com / releases/2011/11/111102093035.htm

Chapter 5

4. Schutte, Dan. "Yahweh, I Know You Are Near." © 1971 Dan Schutte & New Dawn Music.

5   Odendaal, J.S.J. and R.A. Meintjes. "Neurophysiological Correlates of Affiliative Behavior Between Humans and Dogs." Veterinary Journal 165: (2003): 296-301.

6. Olmert, Meg Daley. *Made for Each Other: The Biology of the Human-Animal Bond*. Cambridge, 2009. Xvii.

Chapter 6

7. American Veterinary Society of Animal Behavior. "Position Statement on Puppy Socialization." 2008 Retrieved online 4/17/2013 from http://avsabonline.org/ uploads/position_statements/puppy_socialization1-25-13.pdf.

Chapter 7

8. Susan Nolen-Hoeksema, Blair E. Wisco, Sonja Lyubomirsky. "Rethinking Rumination." Perspectives on Psychological Science. Vol. 3, No. 5. September 2008. Retrieved online 4/17/2003 from http://pps.sagepub.com/content/3/5/400.abstract

9. Lyon Ranch Therapy Animals founders Robin and Robert Lyon seek to enrich lives through the healing power of animals. More information on Lyon Ranch Therapy Animals can be found at www.lyonranch.org.

10. "Mission." Gabriel's Angels, Pets Helping Kids website. Retrieved online 4/24/2013 from http://www.gabrielsangels.org/about_mission.php. CEO Pat Gaber is the author of *Gabriel's Angels—The Story of the Dog Who Inspired a Revolution*, which tells the story of the agency.

Chapter 8

11.   Horowitz, Alexandra. *Inside of a Dog.* 2009.

Chapter 9

12.   Wilson, E.O. *Biophilia.* 1984.

13.   Louv, Richard. *Last Child in the Woods: Saving Our Children from Nature-Deficit Disorder.* 2005

14.   Louv, Richard. *The Nature Principle.* 2011.

15.   Selhub, Eva and Alan Logan. *Your Brain On Nature: The Science of Nature's Influence on Your Health, Happiness and Vitality.* 2012.